Praise for *Perfect, Once Removed*

"When I pitched a perfect game against the Dodgers in the 1956 World Series, I knew my life had changed. But I had no idea that, back in Indiana, the game had also turned things around for my nine-year-old cousin, Phil. Though *Perfect, Once Removed* is about the connection between Phil and me, I think what the book really shows is the huge pull that baseball has always had on kids. It's a wonderful story and I'm glad Phil wrote it."

—Don Larsen

"Disguised as a nostalgic, coming-of-age baseball memoir, this is a sly, spare meditation on the perils of childhood, the power of celebrity, the vagaries of human kindness, and how even tenuous family bonds can have a surprisingly steely impact."

—Joe Pilla, Paperbacks Plus, Bronx, NY

"Hoose vividly captures not only a *Leave It to Beaver* world that is gone forever, but also the timeless romance between a boy and baseball (the book's subtitle is "When Baseball Was All the World to Me." Who can't relate?). And he does so in a sweet but clear-eyed way that never gets overly sentimental."

—Nick Cristiano, *Philadelphia Inquirer*

"*Perfect, Once Removed* is not so much about the magic of that golden afternoon in Yankee Stadium as it is the magic of baseball when the game wraps itself around a boy's soul…[Hoose's] recollections are tinged with just the right amount of exuberance and self-deprecation. The book's publisher likens Hoose's storytelling to Jean Shepherd's, and the comparison is not, shall we say, off-base. Substitute an A2000 fielder's glove for a Red Ryder BB gun, and you get the idea…No errors here."

—John Carney, *Boston Globe*

"This endearing memoir is like a large slice of delicious lemon meringue pie delivered at a small town Indiana church supper. Mr. Hoose, a cousin of Don Larsen of the perfect World Series game in 1956, starts third grade in a new school that year, has his struggles adjusting, fails at baseball, and yet emerges in part because of a zealous love for his cousin, the Yankees, and above all else our great game. I loved it because, like baseball, it is about failure and ultimate redemption." —**Fay Vincent, former Commissioner of Major League Baseball**

"A wonderful little gem of a baseball memoir...Though *Perfect, Once Removed* has many universal themes relating to baseball, and childhood, and the feeling of being an outsider, that specific connection to Larsen makes the book more than just a paean to the game. It's also history, experienced from a unique viewpoint." —**Jeff Merron**, *108 Magazine*

"Baby boomers love to write about their childhood baseball experiences, and while it's arguable whether later generations feel similar joy when reading these heartfelt recollections, every now and then a nostalgia-soaked boomer steps up to the plate and connects. Hoose is one of those, and his story speaks to every baseball-loving kid whose talent on the field wasn't equal to his passion for the game...No denying it, there was something special about baseball in the fifties, and Hoose nails it as surely as Larsen mowed down those twenty-seven Dodgers." —**Bill Ott**, *Booklist* **(starred review)**

"Teens will appreciate this story of an ordinary boy and his brush with real superheroes. Hoose met Larsen and such Yankee greats as Yogi Berra and Casey Stengel; he saw the loner Mickey Mantle from across the room. In a satisfying close to this story, the author visits with his now eighty-year-old cousin. Period photos help readers to visualize the times."

—Will Marston, *Library Journal*

"Endearing…With consummate skill Mr. Hoose evokes the era of apple pie and white picket fences, but his book is more than just a period piece. His portrait of a boy's passion for baseball will ring true to anyone who has ever listened to a game on the radio after lights out or engaged in the oft-argued debate about whether the gum that came with baseball cards was, in fact, tasty. His tale is as enduring as Don Larsen was flawless that one afternoon 50 years ago." **—Eric Wills**, *Washington Times*

"Hoose weaves an ode to childhood and baseball that is close to perfect." **—Bryan French**, *Fort Worth Star-Telegram*

"Wonderful…A warm and honest portrait…a gem of a memoir."
—*Tallahassee Democrat*

"Hoose's genuine passion for the game shines through…and the self-effacing descriptions of his boyhood troubles make you want to root, root, root for the kid with the big glasses and the wild arm. Removed from perfect indeed, but all the more charming for it." **—***Kirkus Reviews*

PERFECT,

ONCE REMOVED

WHEN BASEBALL WAS
ALL THE WORLD TO ME

PHILLIP HOOSE

Walker & Company
New York

Published by Walker Publishing Company, Inc., New York
Distributed to the trade by Macmillan

All papers used by Walker & Company are natural, recyclable products made from wood grown in well-managed forests. The manufacturing processes conform to the environmental regulations of the country of origin.

Art credits Page 70: postcard from the collection of Richard A. Johnson.
Pages 89 and 155: photographs by Richard Connelly.
Pages 110 and 133: Corbis. Page 151: photograph by Corinne Larsen.
Page 159: photograph by Wendell Clough.
All other images courtesy of the author.

LIBRARY OF CONGRESS CATALOGING–IN–PUBLICATION DATA HAS BEEN APPLIED FOR.

ISBN-10: 0-8027-1537-0 (hardcover)
ISBN-13: 978-0-8027-1537-1 (hardcover)

Visit Walker & Company's Web site at www.walkerbooks.com

First published by Walker & Company in 2006
This paperback edition published in 2008

Paperback ISBN-10: 0-8027-1627-x
ISBN-13: 978-0-8027-1627-9

2 4 6 8 10 9 7 5 3 1

Typeset by Westchester Book Group
Printed in the United States of America by Quebecor World Fairfield

Building an Ark: Tools for the Preservation of Natural Diversity through Land Protection

Hoosiers: The Fabulous Basketball Life of Indiana

Necessities: Racial Barriers in American Sports

It's Our World, Too: Young People Who Are Making a Difference

Hey, Little Ant (with Hannah Hoose)

We Were There, Too: Young People in U.S. History

The Race to Save the Lord God Bird

To the memory of

Oreal Brown, Kahlo Larsen, and Lincoln C. Northcott,

wonderful men who

I wish I could have known much longer

Much of the dialogue in the following pages is re-created because I am not able to remember the exact words of my family, friends, and acquaintances of fifty years ago. It is however entirely accurate as to what was said and how it was said.

CHAPTER ONE

DECEMBER 1955

"I'm working on a new idea . . . The automobile is at the dawn of a great development . . . We are coming into a fast-moving age and the old horse can't go the pace. Wouldn't it be a great idea to build a horseless city just opposite the Indianapolis Motor Speedway, an industrial city devoted to the motorization of all traffic?"

CARL G. FISHER, FOUNDER OF THE INDIANAPOLIS
MOTOR SPEEDWAY, 1909

I STARED OUT the window of our Plymouth at the crusty snow banked up on both sides of the street as we pulled up to a small, square white house with a bare maple tree in front. Dad folded the map and stuffed it in the glove compartment. Mom put lipstick on. 1738 Allison Street, Speedway, Indiana. Right next to Indianapolis. My new home.

The house was freezing. We kept our coats and mittens on while Dad shoveled coal into the furnace downstairs, then got back in the car to explore the town while the house heated up. The snow-narrowed streets in our neighborhood, the old section of town, were lined with small, one-storied wooden houses like ours. Dad pointed out that the streets were named after old cars—Ford, Auburn, Cord, and Winton. A few minutes later, we entered a neighborhood of low ranch houses separated by generous lawns from "drives." They were named after newer cars with higher tailfins—DeSoto, Cadillac, Lincoln, and Imperial.

Dad had moved us into a sort of theme park. Maybe other Indiana towns had been built along waterways and railroads by settlers who needed to get grain to market, but Speedway had been "designed" by four engineers. Their names—names that I would later memorize for credit—were Carl G. Fisher, James A. Allison, Arthur C. Newby, and Frank H. Wheeler. Their moment of inspiration had arrived in a restaurant one night in 1907. As they were dining and dreaming, their leader, Carl G. Fisher, withdrew a pencil from his shirt pocket and smoothed out a napkin on the table. The others leaned forward. Fisher scrawled a large oval and looked up. That, he informed his companions, perhaps tapping his pencil, was the future.

Fisher's oval was the shape of the colossal track they would build, two and a half miles around, where all the great new automobiles of the day could be tested, tinkered with, improved, redesigned, and, of course, raced. Indianapolis was rapidly becoming one of America's leading auto-making cities, and Fisher had grown up nearby. They bought a flat piece of land a few miles west of the city and broke ground on the track. After a while, the visionaries realized that they would need a town to go with their oval, a place where the men who ground out engine parts and clicked stopwatches could raise future engineers and mechanics. They laid out the first streets in careful grids. Fisher called it "Speedway City," but it was later incorporated simply as the town of Speedway.

And now, forty-eight years after Fisher's vision, I, eight-year-old Phil Hoose, son of Darwin Hoose, an aircraft engineer one year out of college and three years out of Korea, and his wife, Patty—at this moment feeling betrayed and bitterly disappointed that we had not started post-college life in California as she believed she had been promised—had come to live in Carl G. Fisher's valentine to the internal combustion engine.

Anything in Speedway that wasn't named after a racecar was named after one of the four guys at the table. I would be going to Carl G. Fisher school, that is until the Arthur C. Newby school was finished. Had I been born two years later and lived in a different part of town, I would have attended the Frank H. Wheeler Elementary School. I would live on Allison Street and my dad would work at the Allison Division of General Motors. The high school sports team was called the Sparkplugs. The chorus was the Sparkleaires, the school yearbook the Speedette. The car motif saturated everything. It was like a comedian with only one joke. I would come to learn that nobody ever got tired of it.

Headed east along Crawfordsville Road, Dad turned the Plymouth onto Georgetown Road. On the right, tapering off into a horizon all its own, loomed the gray grandstands of the Indianapolis Motor Speedway. Dad said the Indianapolis 500 Mile Race—a car race held each year on my birthday weekend—attracted more people than any other sporting event in the world. When May came, he said, I would see more people than I could imagine, and they would come from all over the world. I might get to meet a few of them, too, since it looked like maybe we lived close enough to the track to make a few bucks parking cars on our lawn. The reason, he said, that so many businesses decorated their buildings in a black-and-white checkered pattern was that these were the colors of the flag that ended the race.

I smeared a circle of frost away and pressed my nose against the back window. Bleachers went on for miles, behind a hurricane fence interrupted by numbered gates every few hundred yards. Fields across from the track had been paved into parking lots, with signs poking out of the snow to attract cars and mobile homes even in the dead of winter.

As we swung back toward home, I blew on the window and traced my name in the fog. In South Bend, where we had lived before, there had been rivers and hills. Here the roads were ruler-straight and the land was as flat as the top of a table. Who cared about cars? All I knew was that I spent too much time stuck in the backseat of one. I had seen enough. I wanted to go back to South Bend.

On the first school day of 1956, the students of Carl G. Fisher Elementary School milled around on the lawn, throwing snow-balls and chasing each other until a bell sounded, at which moment two teachers pulled back the front doors and stepped aside. Speedway's grade-schoolers stampeded in through the arched doorway and clomped up a flight of stairs, jostling my mom and me as they surged toward their classrooms. Heat pipes sputtered and coughed as we veered off into the school office to enroll me as a third-grade student.

After Mom filled out the forms, a secretary ushered us in to see the principal, who stood up from his desk. He was a short, stocky man with thinning black hair combed straight back from his forehead, steel-rimmed glasses, and a mouth full of silver fillings. He had the jowls of a bulldog. The plate on his desk said LIN-COLN C. NORTHCOTT, PRINCIPAL. He spoke to Mom but kept his eyes on me. "You'll like this town, Mrs. Hoose," he was saying. "It's a good town. Phillip will enjoy this school. He has a fine teacher in Mrs. Perrigo." The pale sun glinted off his glasses, concealing his eyes, but I didn't need to see them. Everything about him said, "Stay out of this office, kid, if you know what's good for you."

Mom lingered a moment to say good-bye to me in the hall. Normally Mom looked pretty, but right then she looked tired. So was I, and she knew it. This was my fourth school in three years. After he had come back from Korea, Dad kept moving us around, from South Bend to an even smaller town named Angola where he went to college, then back to South Bend, and now this car town. As a family, we were wrung out. Mom knelt down and smoothed my shirt. "You're gonna like it here, honey," she said, doing her best to smile. "I know, Mom," I said, doing my best not to cry. I stood in the hall and watched her disappear down the stairs and out the front doors. A secretary took me by the wrist and tugged me in the opposite direction.

When the door opened, my third-grade classroom froze. The teacher, Mrs. Perrigo, was in the middle of an arithmetic lesson.

She put her chalk down, smiled tightly, thanked the secretary, and beckoned for me to stand before the class in the middle of the room.

"We have a new student, class. Say your name, please."

"Phil Hoose."

Someone tittered. It's pronounced *hose,* even though it's spelled like it should rhyme with *moose.* Don't ask me why. My grandpa always said Roosevelt had the same problem until people got used to him. I could feel thirty sets of eyes looking me up and down, inspecting my posture, grading my clothing, scrutinizing my expression, metering my confidence. I stood before them wearing polished cotton trousers hiked up several inches above the waist and a checkered shirt buttoned to the top. My shoes were white bucks, because that's what Pat Boone wore. Each of my new classmates was already completing a verdict from which there would be no appeal. I could have saved them the trouble and written it on the board: "Phil Hoose: Small. Wears glasses. Big butt. Bad haircut. Weird name." Wordlessly, each was asking: "Will I have to move over in any way to make room for this new kid?" As I slid past them to my desk in the back of the room, I felt the answer rising like a slow sigh of steam from the radiator. It was a unanimous "no."

The next weeks proved them right. I had assets, all right, but none of them amounted to much. I was as good as the best girls in spelldowns. I was a valuable teammate in a flashcard competition. Because I had a big mouth, I could irritate Mrs. Perrigo, and that did count for something. But being a wisecracker also made me enemies, and I had no brothers or sisters to cover my backside in a tight situation. I was extremely nearsighted and not brave and not strong. They all said I talked funny, but that was because they couldn't hear themselves. When they said "push," it came out "poo-ish." "Wish" was "woosh." "Motel" was "MO-tel." "Defrost" was "DE-frost." "Special" came out "spatial." Some of the sounds they made I couldn't understand at all. Ignoring my peril, I mocked them.

Actually, I tried to keep my mouth shut, but I was just mouthy by nature. Mine was a toxic combination, weak and mouthy. I seemed to arouse the deepest homicidal tendencies of one kid in particular, a pale, wiry boy named Stan Purdue. I guess I awakened in him the pure joy of stalking. I would first sense his presence behind me on the way home from school as I approached Sixteenth Street, a few blocks from Fisher. His footsteps flushed me into an ever-quickening pace, which became an all-out sprint for home and finally a pounce, with him landing on top of me and forcing my face down in the snow. My glasses never stayed on. "You're gonna pay for thith, Purdue," I'd sputter through the snow in my mouth. That got me more snow in the mouth.

One day I got up from such a beating, scooped up a double armload of snow, walked inside our house, and dumped the snow onto the living room carpet. My mom just stood there, blinking. "Why would you *do* that, Phillip?" she asked me. I had no way to tell her that I needed to get back at someone and she was the only one I felt safe in provoking. Livid, she chased me around the tiny rooms. "Wait'll your dad gets home!" she panted. Nothing happened when Dad got home; by then the anger had drained from both Mom and me. When I told Dad about Stan Purdue,

I could sense his disappointment. I should be tougher. By now I should be able to take care of myself. He told me about the mocking idiot who had followed him home every day at Nooner School in South Bend—that is, until Dad wheeled and decked him with a stiff right. "Great, Dad," I said. "Why don't you come to school tomorrow and we'll find Purdue so you can show me how you did it."

At night, I dreamed I was a dirigible. I had a knob that grew out of my hip. When I twisted it, air escaped from me and I rose. Whenever Stan Purdue jumped out from behind a tree with an iceball cocked in his fist, I rose so high so fast that I couldn't even hear him scream "chicken" or "moron." Some nights I flew back to see my grandpa in South Bend or out to California to see my Uncle Art and Aunt Gladys. But most nights I just hovered around Speedway, accepting my fate and lowering myself back to the snow only when I was sure Stan Purdue had slunk back to whatever cave he lived in.

By February, a faint glow of pale light had already reached my bedroom window by the time Dad came in to wake me up for school. With each day, stronger light pooled in the arched windows of our old school building and gleamed off the polished maple planks of our classroom floor. And as winter gave way to spring, each member of the Hoose family sent down thin, persistent roots into the permafrost of Speedway society. My mom became a den mother, thus making me a Cub Scout. Dad bought a green corduroy suit at Robert Hall and joined a carpool of pipe-smoking engineers. They drove waving off to work in the morning in one high-finned car or another. Sometimes they dropped me off at school.

In March, on the first really warm day of the year, Mrs. Perrigo unlocked a closet and stood aside as the boys swarmed around a cardboard box. Someone pulled out a bat and ball and led the others down the schoolhouse steps and outside. They ran past the asphalt playground where we had played dodgeball all winter, and streamed out onto a muddy field. Wearing rubber boots, I trudged along behind, looking around and saying nothing. I had never noticed the baseball diamond before, since it had been covered in snow all winter. By the time I got there, they had already named captains, chosen sides, and taken their positions. I walked to the distant patch of ground where someone told me to stand. Luckily, no one hit a ball anywhere near me.

I was leaning against a fence when someone said it was my turn to bat. The bat was black and chipped and very heavy. I had never played baseball. Back in South Bend at recess, we had just chased girls around or climbed on things. We didn't have any official games. My grandpa was always begging me to watch baseball games with him on TV, but you needed a saddle to sit on Grandpa Brown's lap during a ballgame. He yelled and coughed and swore at the umpires. Suddenly I wished I had paid attention. I didn't even know the rules of baseball, but I could see I had better learn fast. Clearly this was what we were going to do at recess every day until summer vacation. I couldn't stay behind and skip rope with the girls, not and stay alive with the boys.

A classmate turned my hands around on the bat and helped me

hoist it into something like a hitting position. He backed away and someone tossed the ball underhanded in my direction. I flung the bat toward it and lurched in front of the plate, barely keeping my balance. I did it twice more and let the bat drop onto the soggy ground. Once again I heard the word "moron."

At dinner I steered green beans around my plate with my fork and told my parents what had happened. Mom lit a cigarette. Dad frowned. Nobody said much for a while. Then Dad scraped back his chair and told me to go grab my jacket. We drove to Sears and bought a bat, two gloves, and a ball. I knew it cost a lot of money for us right then, but we were all making adjustments and Dad knew I needed these tools every bit as much as he needed his slide rule and Mom needed her Scout manual. Baseball equipment was an investment, plain and simple.

When we got home, Dad and I went out back and paced a few feet apart in the slushy ground. The bright orange J. C. Higgins glove felt stiff and foreign on my left hand. It looked like a lobster claw. I couldn't close it. Dad threw softly, underhanded, his pipe clenched between his teeth. The third toss struck the heel of the glove, rolled up my arm, and hit me in the face. I started sniffling.

"Keep your eye on the ball," Dad said.

"Where do you think it was?" I yelled, rubbing my cheekbone.

I picked up the ball and flung it back at him as hard as I could, trying to throw it through him. It looped over his shoulder, which made me madder. Dad gave me a quizzical look. I hated him right then. "Put your *pipe* away," I yelled, my face still stinging and my vision blurring with tears. "You can't play ball and smoke a pipe." Dad knew a whole lot about a lot of things, but I could see right then that he didn't know a bit more about baseball than I did. How could he? He had only been nine when his own dad died, and there had been no one to teach him. He'd had no brothers or sisters. In the years that he should have been learning to hit and throw, he was scrubbing floors with my grandma.

But if Dad couldn't teach me, and if I had no friends, how was I going to learn to play this stupid game?

The next day, I squeezed in between two engineers and motored off to school with Dad's car pool. These guys all wore suits and fedoras and white shirts with plastic pocket protectors. They talked in a language all their own though pipe-clenched teeth. Collectively they emitted a sticky blue haze that flattened and spread around the dome light. They were like squids. You could barely breathe in that car.

Actually, I was a little unclear about what Dad did for a living. Lacking a "security clearance," I couldn't visit his office at Allison Plant Eight, and I never would. All I knew was that he went off with these guys and worked on jet airplane engines. Sometimes he stayed away when there were "engine tests." His work was something you weren't supposed to ask much about, not if you loved your country.

Though Dad usually joined in the banter with the other

engineers in the car, on this morning he was silent all the way to school. I figured he was thinking about me. When we pulled up to Fisher and I got out, he called me back to the car. Through the window he looked into my eyes and said, firmly, "Never stop running." This was his advice about baseball. He smiled and winked, and I stepped back from the curb and the engineers sped away. I repeated the words as the bell rang and I joined the stampede into the building. Never stop running. It sounded like gold to me.

Two hours later at recess, I once again lifted the bat to my shoulder and watched another pitch float toward me. I swung with all my strength and felt a tingle of contact in my arms and hands. Looking down, I saw the ball rolling slowly in the direction of the pitcher, who seemed as startled as I was. My brain sent a signal to my legs that it was time to start running, so I took off, with Dad's words filling my ears. "Never stop running! Never stop running!" Head down, I churned toward first in my mud-caked galoshes, dragging the bat behind me. I didn't see the pitcher pick up the ball and toss it underhand to the kid playing first base. As I rounded first and churned toward second, still trailing the bat, my breath came in ragged gasps. Above the pounding of my heart I could hear my Dad's words. It seemed like the kids were screaming something, too. They sounded as excited as I was.

The first baseman's throw probably reached second long before I did, but I didn't notice. By then I was on my way to third. The bat felt like a suitcase and my lungs were on fire and my legs were weakening, but I wasn't going to stop. Never. Dad was really on to something here—wait'll he heard about this! The ball awaited me at third as I wheezed by and it was there at home too as I closed in on the plate. The catcher braced himself and upon my arrival shoved me sprawling into the mud, the ball still in his hand. He raised it above his head in leering triumph as I lay gasping before him. The sounds of laughter soared over my pounding heart. "Four outs on one play!" they were saying. "All by himself! A new record for Hoose! What a moron!!!"

CHAPTER TWO

I FOUND OUT about my famous cousin almost by accident one day. Mom and Dad and I were driving home from church. I was alone in the backseat, surrounded by a small mountain of baseball magazines, cards, and books. Part of my new strategy for learning to play baseball was to *read* everything possible about it. My parents gave me pre-birthday subscriptions to *Sport* magazine and *Baseball Digest,* and I devoured each week's *Sporting News* at the Speedway Library. I was soon wearing the librarians out, borrowing the works of my literary idol John R. Tunis and returning them on extremely short rotations. All his books were immortal, but the best by far—the greatest book ever written—far better than the more popular *The Kid from Tompkinsville*—was *Highpockets.* It was the story of Cecil McDade, a tremendously talented rookie centerfielder for the Brooklyn Dodgers who is also an obnoxious braggart. His teammates can't stand him. Then he gets in a car crash and everyone learns important life lessons. Pulling together, the Dodgers race off with the National League pennant and McDade gets Rookie-of-the-Year.

It was fabulous. I could read a John R. Tunis a day, and sometimes did.

Head buried in a *Baseball Digest* as we moved along Sixteenth Street, I was sounding off to no one in particular about how hard it was to learn this dumb game. Grounders came up in your face. Popups came down on your head. Why couldn't the various people who stitched the baseballs slip in a little padding? I'd like to see one of *them* take a bad hop or two. Why didn't people stop telling me to "choke up" on the bat? If I choked up any farther, I'd jab myself in the stomach when I swung. Why did everybody have a head start on me? Why hadn't anyone taught me before now? It wasn't fair. It wasn't right. Speaking of Sunday school, where was God in all this? Why did we have to move here anyway? *What kind of parents would stick me in a situation like this?*

Mom lowered the radio and turned around. "Why don't you ask your cousin about it?" she said, dropping the words lightly, as if she were flicking an ash out the car window.

"What cousin?"

"Don Larsen, your Dad's cousin . . . Ask *him* about baseball. Darwin, who does Don play for now? Darwin?"

"The Yankees," my dad said absently.

"There," said Mom, turning back around.

I studied the backs of their heads. My parents liked a good laugh as much as anyone, but they weren't exactly pranksters. Mom had one joke she told whenever we passed a cemetery. "How many people are dead there?" she would ask us. After an instant's pause, she'd answer, "All of them." It broke her up.

Likewise Dad enjoyed a chortle now and then, but neither seemed capable of the elaborate planning required to tell me on the way home from church that I had a cousin in the major leagues, and then to keep a straight face. Besides, it would be cruel, and they weren't cruel. They loved me. On the other hand, this couldn't possibly be true. If it were, how could they have kept it from me? This was news on the order of a cure for polio or that the Russians had converted to freedom.

I fumbled through my stack of books and reached for *The Official Baseball Encyclopedia* (Revised Edition), edited by Hy Turkin and S. C. Thompson, which I kept with me at all times. I looked in the "All-Time Register" for "Don Larson," but found nothing. How could my parents have done this to me? Then my finger settled on an entry for "Don Larsen." It began:

Larsen, Donald James
b. Aug. 7, 1929, Michigan City, Ind. BR TR 6'4" 215 lbs.

My mind connected the dots: "Larsen"—that's how Grandma Larsen spelled her name. Jennie too. Uncle Art too. Uncle Kay too. 1929—that was only three years younger than Dad. Michigan City—that was near South Bend, and I knew we were supposed to have relatives from Michigan City. Hadn't I heard my grandma talk about Jim and Lottie from Michigan City? And their daughter Joyce—hadn't we called her "Joyce of the Secret Squadron"? On paper, this actually seemed possible. I put the book down and studied the backs of my parents' heads. No conspiratorial sideways glances, no winks, no stifled giggles. I looked at Dad's face in the rearview mirror. His eyes were straight on the road.

I hoisted myself forward and planted my arms on the back of the front seat. "Dad, don't joke about this. Do you really have a cousin who is a major league baseball player?"

"Well, yeah. Crimenetly."

"Do you *know* him?"

"Well, yeah, just like you know your cousin Mike."

"Jesus Christ, Dad . . ."

Their heads snapped around and the car swerved to the left. "Don't you *ever* say that again, Phillip."

That always got them: Taking the Lord's Name in Vain. They themselves never actually did it, but it was amazing how close they could come to saying "Jesus Christ" without saying it. My dad could hit his thumb with a hammer and yelp "Crime*tly*!!!" but it didn't count. My mom could burn a pork chop and yell "Oh, for Cripes SAKE!" but that didn't count either. Neither did "Key-*Ripes*."

Anyway, now that I had their attention, I got them to tell me that Don Larsen was my great-uncle Jim's son. Joyce of the Secret Squadron's brother. Uncle Jim was my Grandma Hoose's brother. Grandma Hoose was of course my dad's mother. That made Don Larsen my dad's first cousin, and therefore my cousin once removed, or my second cousin. Dad said that the Larsens— Jim, Lottie, Joyce, and Don—had moved away from Indiana to California when Don was about fourteen and my dad seventeen. Then Dad had gone away to World War II and they hadn't seen each other much after that, except for a brief visit when Dad was stationed in San Diego.

Mom held up her left hand. "Don's dad made my wedding ring," she said. "He's a jeweler."

It looked like an ordinary wedding ring.

"How good was he, Dad?"

"Oh, he was very good. He could make necklaces, earrings, rings, anything."

"That isn't what I mean, Dad."

"Well, what *do* you mean?"

"Baseball. Did you ever play baseball with Don Larsen?"

"Sure, we played catch out at the cottage. We were out there one whole summer working for Dutch." My uncle Dutch had bought a small cottage on the St. Joseph River in South Bend, where Dad's side of the family sometimes gathered on summer weekends.

"What do you remember about it?"

"About what?

"About playing catch with Don Larsen!"

"I remember that he was a kid."

My dad began puffing on his pipe. As I pressed in, a thickening cloud swirled around his head, rose to the dome light, and coated the car's ceiling.

"How *fast* was he, Dad? How hard could he throw?"

I wanted Dad to tell me that one afternoon they were playing catch out at the cottage and Don got a little irritated for some reason Dad still didn't understand and fired one back so hard that it bent Dad's fingers back double and dislocated one of them. That, he could have explained, holding up his hand, is why this finger here is crooked. But there were no such stories, and his fingers were straight anyway. No, all I got from Dad was more pipe smoke. He seemed mildly annoyed by the conversation, as if I had pulled him out of a daydream. As I pressed on for details, Dad started to whistle. He mainly knew two songs, "Tenderly" and "They Tried to Tell Us We're too Young," both from World War II. Both meant the same thing: end of conversation.

I returned to the *Baseball Encyclopedia* and examined Don Larsen's statistical record. He had broken in with the St. Louis Browns in 1953. His rookie year, he won seven games and lost twelve. Yes, it was ugly, but his team had finished last so I reckoned it wasn't his fault. But the next year, with Baltimore in 1954, my brand-new cousin had won three games and lost *twenty-one*. I put my hand to my mouth. That was the worst record I had ever heard of. Why would any team keep a pitcher that bad? Why would a manager ever give a pitcher a chance to lose twenty-one games? But then it got truly weird. The next year, which was the previous season, 1955, he had inexplicably been traded to the New York Yankees, kings of baseball. He spent the first half of the year in the minors, and then got called up to New York. And there, supported by Mickey Mantle, Yogi Berra, and Hank Bauer, he had mutated into a different species, winning nine games and losing only two. Obviously, somebody must have seen something good in him and gambled on him. Looked like they got it right.

I watched the freshly budding trees whiz by out the back window of the Plymouth and tried to make the whole thing add up: Don Larsen, pitcher for the New York Yankees. Don Larsen, my cousin (once removed).

The *Baseball Encyclopedia* said he weighed three times as much as me and stood a foot and a half taller. But if this was true, what did it matter? Somehow, unless my parents were pulling the Hoax of the Century, a major league baseball player's blood flowed through my veins. We were kin, connected by tradition and places and people in common. Since Dad said Don had been to the cottage, that meant that, like me, he had stepped onto the highest stone, removed the thick rope from the nail that held it against a tree, grabbed it, taken a step backward, and swung yelling out over the St. Joseph River just like me. Like me, he had waited until the farthest point and dropped, kicking and maybe holding his nose just like me, into the green, cold water. Donald James Larsen might have had an earned run average of 3.06 but he also probably knew that my grandma could float on her back. He had played catch with my dad, and his dad made my mom's wedding ring. He knew Uncle Dutch and he knew Uncle Kay and, the bottom line was, he had to help me. He had no choice. Blood was blood.

When we got home, I called Grandma Hoose in South Bend. "Don? Well, sure, honey, didn't anybody ever tell you about him? Jim and Lottie's son. They moved out to California, but he's still a nice boy." Later, Grandma called back with an address for him, in care of the Yankees. Without delay I wrote the following letter:

Dear Don Larsen. My Dad, Darwin Hoose, says you're his cousin. That makes you my cousin too. I've just started playing baseball. It's my first season. I'm having a horrible time learning. Do you have any advice?

Sincerely,

Phil Hoose (Darwin's son)

CHAPTER THREE

WASHINGTON (AP) APRIL 17, 1956

After President Eisenhower threw out the first pitch of the season, Mickey Mantle grabbed the spotlight by blasting two homers over the center field fence at Griffith Stadium, marking the first time in history any slugger has cleared the distant barrier twice in a single game to help power the Yankees to a 10–4 victory over the Washington Senators. Mr. Eisenhower remained for the entire contest and joined with the crowd of 27,837 in cheering Mickey's wallops off Washington hurler Camilo Pascual in the first and sixth innings. Yogi Berra also homered, and, in addition, collected a double and two singles for five RBIs. The work of the powerhouse pair made pitching easy for Don Larsen, who breezed to the win with a six-hitter.

THE FIRST REPLY was a postcard dated May 17, 1956. Don Larsen's photo was on one side and his message to me on the other. The postmark showed it had been mailed just before midnight from somewhere in Chicago. I imagined Don telling Mantle and Berra to wait up a second while he hustled over to the mail slot of a fancy hotel lobby and dropped my postcard in ·

with his right hand. Before reading the message, I studied the photograph. Don was posing as if he had just thrown a pitch. He was trying hard to hold the position; he looked like he had been shot and stuffed in the act of following through.

The great thing about it was that he was wearing the Yankee home uniform, cotton white, with the imperial "NY" sewn proudly on the blouse right over his pinstriped heart. The same insignia was also stitched onto the front of his dark baseball cap, whose bill was shaped perfectly. Don's eyebrows were thick and his ears stuck out. He had a confident expression. I liked it that he wasn't smiling—this showed that he was not a man to mess with. His autograph was scrawled across his knees. It had a southwest-to-northeast slant, and weakened as it went along. This showed that he was way too busy to worry about making all his letters perfect. I liked the way he made his "D" in "Don" a lot.

I turned the postcard over. His message to me was written in blue ink. Brief and to the point, it didn't offer any technical information, but it was encouraging: Addressed to me at 1738 Allison Street in Speedway, it said, "Here's luck on your baseball. I'm rooting for you and maybe I'll get a chance to see you soon." It was signed "Don Larsen." The D on the back matched the D on the front. So it was true: A New York Yankee, someone who

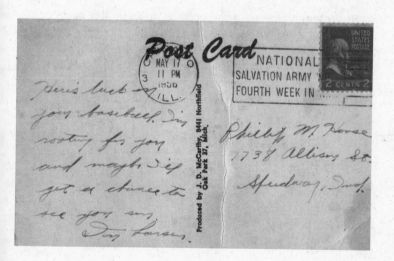

made his living pitching for the greatest baseball team on earth, was rooting for me. He knew my name. He hoped he could see me. Here, at last, was my first real break in baseball.

It would have made a lot more sense if Don Larsen had been my mom's cousin. Dad's people—the Larsens—were big-boned Norwegians who loved noisy canasta games and bottles of beer and walleye fishing. They bickered and feuded and laughed out loud and floated on their backs, but as far as I knew, none of them cared a whit about team sports.

By contrast, playing baseball was a sacred activity for the Browns, my mom's people. It had been this way since at least the 1880s, when Ben Brown, my great-grandfather, caught bare-handed for a team in Carbon, Indiana, a coal-mining community about forty miles northeast of Terre Haute, where he moved with his family. The area had become a magnet for coal companies when the New York Central railroad was laid over a thick seam of bituminous coal in western Indiana. By 1895, the year my grandpa Oreal Brown was born, Carbon had four thousand people, thirteen saloons, and several dozen deep mines. Every mine had a baseball team.

Like many boys around Carbon, Grandpa quit school and went down in the mines as soon as he could, hiring on as a mule driver for the Eberhardt Coal Company at the age of fourteen. As he sat on the front bumper of a coal car, whip in hand and staring through the gloom at the slowly shifting flanks and switching tail of his mule, he dreamed about playing third base. That was the position he took over for the Eberhardt nine shortly after he was hired. The best day of the week was Saturday, the day of the games, when he walked to the diamond with his dad and played until dark.

The Army and World War I shattered any dreams Grandpa might have had for pro ball. He survived the slaughter in Europe and came home to more death. Spanish influenza, the world-wide epidemic incubated in the army camps of Europe, had already reached Carbon. By the winter of 1919, the Carbon cemetery had been expanded several times to hold the newly dead. Grandpa watched his father and then his older brother John slip away, gasping and wheezing in the final hours, "foaming like a steam engine," as one sister wrote. Grandpa's nieces and nephews, aunts and cousins and friends died as well. Then Grandpa got the flu, too, mild at first and rapidly more severe as pneumonia developed. His sisters lowered him again and again into a zinc tub filled with freezing water to bring down his temperature. Grandpa survived with a permanently weakened lung, an organ that he punished all the rest of his life with coal dust and unfiltered Camels. He never stopped coughing.

The family's baseball hopes shifted to my mom's older bother Tom Brown, born in Carbon while Grandpa was in Verdun. Uncle Tom's ability was obvious from the start. A natural catcher, Tom was described as tough, hard-hitting, durable—and charming. Crouching behind them, Tom distracted batters with an improvised, never-ending story about a little red rooster. His narrative went on for years, and became increasingly elaborate. No one could make him stop—and some probably didn't want him to.

Friday was the day Grandpa and Tom would go into Carbon to charge the battery, a three-volt Atwater Kent that powered just about everything before electricity. The next afternoon, Grandpa would place the battery and a speaker on the ground and toss cables back to Tom through the living room window for connection to the family radio. Grandpa went back inside and fiddled with the dial, hacking and swearing until he found KMOX, a 50,000-watt clear-channel station originating in St. Louis. Then Tom and Grandpa would settle back for the weekly dose of their beloved Cardinals. Curled at their feet was Rip, the beagle Grandpa had named after Cardinal first sacker Rip Collins. It was a Brown family law that no matter what, some battery power had to be saved for Saturday afternoon and the Cardinals.

Uncle Tom was a teenager the day Babe Ruth came to Terre Haute for a "batting exhibition." The Babe was fat and washed up then, nominally a coach with the Brooklyn Dodgers, but with a bat in his hands he was still Babe Ruth. Grandpa and Tom sat open-mouthed in the bleachers as the Babe, whom Tom later remembered as wearing house slippers and with a towel draped around his neck, effortlessly belted pitch after pitch in towering arcs halfway to Indianapolis. It looked like he was hitting golf balls at a driving range. When the Babe had had enough, he headed toward the dugout for refreshment. A fair percentage of the boys in Terre Haute were waiting along the dugout roof as he approached. Uncle Tom vaulted over a couple of backs and stuck a baseball out as far as he could. "Wouldja sign it, Babe?" Tom shouted. The Babe looked up. "Hell, yes, keed," he replied, unscrewing his own fountain pen. "I'll write all over it if you want me to."

Tom Brown (second from right in front row), captain and catcher for his Brazil, Indiana, American Legion team in the mid-1930s

Tom Brown ended up catching for a semipro team in East Chicago. He played well enough to attract a feeler from the Pittsburgh Pirates, but it came too late. Homesick and in love, he went back to Carbon to work in the clay mines and start a family of his own. By then, the rest of the family had moved to South Bend, where Grandpa had found work. None of his next three children—all girls—turned out to be ballplayers, but he came up with one last chance. Grandpa named his younger son—born long after the others—Lynwood, after Detroit pitcher Lynwood "Schoolboy" Rowe. Rowe had hurled for the Terre Haute Tots when the family still lived in Carbon. Uncle Lynn grew up small in stature, but he had enough talent to merit a post–high school tryout with the Boston Braves. In the end, though, he lost interest in baseball and joined the Army instead.

Down but not out, Grandpa Brown turned to grandchildren. As the first to live near him, I became the object of pressure to at least watch the games with him on Saturday. "Philabuck!" he'd greet me, opening his arms and rubbing my butch until it shone, wrecking my cowlick. "It's the Yankees and Detroit today!" He'd snap the set on and bait me up on his lap with the open package of Beechnut gum in his shirt pocket. But trying to stay on his lap could have been an Olympic event. He swore, smoked, bucked, and mostly coughed. I'd slide down after a few batters. "It's boring, Grandpa," I would say. "C'mon, let's draw cartoons." He would turn back to the game, and then afterward he'd drift out back to tune up the Ford, whose hood always seemed to be open.

I suppose Grandpa Brown had resigned himself to looking at me as just the latest in a parade of missed baseball chances. And I also suppose that on the spring day in 1956 when I arrived from Speedway, begging him to unload everything he knew about baseball—*and right now*—I must have shocked him to his boots.

My talent for irritating Mrs. Perrigo blossomed as the buds swelled and the days grew warmer. At first I had to *do* something to annoy her, like throw a spitball, bother the girl who sat in front of me, or let my desktop slam. But in the final weeks before summer vacation, Mrs. Perrigo and I fine-tuned a wavelength all our own. It got so almost anything I did or said would force steam out of her ears. Just before recess one morning, she finally came to a full whistling boil.

All I did was step up to her desk to ask what page we were

supposed to be on in our workbooks. "What are you doing here, Phillip?" she said, lifting her eyes ever so little. "Why didn't you raise your hand from your desk?"

"I didn't think you could see me."

Her eyes locked on mine. "Don't give me that *look*."

"What look?"

"You know very well what look. Get it off your face *now*."

I actually didn't know what she meant. Somehow, I guess, my face could form a magic expression that crossed some line for her. It was hard to make it go away when I didn't know what it looked like. I stared directly into her eyes without blinking—maybe that would show respect. I didn't really care that much, anyway—her biggest punishment so far was to banish me to the cloak hall. It was quiet in there, a place where you could read in peace, surrounded by sleeves that smelled like wet wool. Sometimes she made me go in there and help one of my classmates with his reading. He was a good guy who read very slowly and stuttered when he read out loud. You could tell how much it embarrassed him. But if you slowed it down and said the words clearly, he was good at sounding things out. I liked working with him.

Suddenly Mrs. Perrigo shot up from her chair, grabbed my wrist, spun me around, and nudged me forward. "Let's go see if Mr. Northcott knows how to take that look off your face."

My heart pounded wildly. "No, no. Look, Mrs. Perrigo, look at me now." I was smiling so hard, I thought my face would break. Too late: She had snapped. I was dead. It was widely believed that Mr. Northcott kept an electric paddle constantly plugged into a socket behind his desk. Others said it was a regular wooden paddle, but he swung it so hard that it *felt* electric. At any rate, everyone agreed that no one who entered his office walked out the same.

I dug my heels into the wooden floor. "You get *down* there," Mrs. Perrigo hissed. As we burst through the office door, the secretaries looked up, startled. She told me to wait at the desk and stormed into Mr. Northcott's office. A moment later, the door reopened and they were both looking out at me. "Thank you, Mrs. Perrigo," the principal said evenly. "Come in, Phillip." Mrs. Perrigo shot a smile back over her shoulder. Mr. Northcott closed the door softly and told me to sit down.

He stood and looked out the window for a while without saying anything, as my eyes darted around for the paddle. I couldn't see it, though all the sockets were visible. Then he turned to me and sighed. "Do you play chess?" "No," I said, startled. "A shame," he said, looking back out the window. "There aren't enough students here who play." After a moment, he turned to me again and studied my face. I prayed that he hadn't caught me looking around for the electric paddle and the outlet.

"They say you're a Yankee fan. Is that right?"

"How'd you know?"

"A principal knows everything, Phil, at least a good one. And Larsen's your cousin, right?"

"Once removed. He's my dad's first cousin, my second."

"He had a bumpy spring, didn't he?"

Whoa. I knew exactly what Mr. Northcott was talking about. It had happened a few weeks before, during spring training. Driving through the Florida darkness about five A.M., Don had slammed his convertible into a telephone pole. Though the car was totaled, Don was unhurt except for a chipped tooth, and unapologetic. Casey Stengel, the Yankee manager, stood up for him, telling reporters, "If Larsen can find something around here to do at that hour, more power to him." Newspaper stories quoted an ex-manager of his who once said, "The only thing Larsen fears is sleep."

About five guys had brought the newspaper report of the Florida wreck to third grade the morning after. "Looks like your great cousin ruined things for everyone," one had said. It was reported that Larsen's "pre-dawn escapades" had caused the Yankee brass to crack down on all the players. Now the Yankees had to report for breakfast by eight and be in uniform by ten fifteen A.M. They had to wear sport jackets in the dining halls and tip the waitresses at least twenty-five cents per meal. I hoped the other Yankees didn't hate him. "Who cares?" I had sniffed. "Doesn't matter to Don. He's a Yankee. All he got was a twenty-dollar fine from the cops. He can pay that easy."

It looked like Mr. Northcott had read about it too. But he wasn't razzing me. Somehow, Mr. Northcott's face and voice didn't match. His expression always looked stern, but his voice was kind. His features just naturally settled down in a bulldog expression. On the other hand, maybe he was suckering me into dropping my guard just before he sizzled me into Reddy Kilowatt. Still, I couldn't help it—when he talked to me, I wasn't scared. Actually, I was glad to be in the office with Mr. Northcott and relieved to be out of Mrs. Perrigo's class. For the next while, we just talked baseball. He followed the big leagues, but I was the player he seemed to care most about. He wondered what it was like for me to learn to play such a complicated game all at once.

I told him I practiced by myself, mostly throwing a rubber ball at a rectangle I had painted on the garage door and fielding the rebounds. I imitated the pitchers I saw on TV. Cinders, my cocker spaniel, was the biggest problem. Whenever I went out to play, she stationed herself at the side of the driveway, eyes bright and butt twitching, ready to make her move whenever I went into my windup. If I threw the ball too slowly, Cinders had just enough time to dart in and snatch it in her slimy mouth before it came back to me. She would race out of my reach, then turn to face me, head low, balanced on her front paws with her rear end stuck up in the air, growling, daring me to come get the wet ball. I would advance slowly, calling her name soothingly until I was inches away. Then I would lunge and she would bound away like lightning, with me screaming at her. I made up games to practice every aspect of baseball alone. I threw flies to myself. I invented "roofball," tossing the ball up onto the slanted garage roof and then trying to guess where it would roll down and bound off the gutter.

"But, Phil," Mr. Northcott said, "there's only so much you can learn by yourself. Don't you think you need to play with others to really improve?"

"Yeah, but no one will play with me now. I'm too new. I'm gonna try out for Little League in the summer."

He looked out the window again and then turned back. "Look . . . Mrs. Perrigo was pretty upset a little while ago. I don't know exactly what happened, but she doesn't get like that much. Can you try to keep the peace with her? You'll be doing us both a favor. I know it's hard to be new, especially starting in the middle of the year, but we only have a few weeks of school left till summer. If it gets too much for you, you can come down here and stay with me for a while. I think we can work this out together. Will you try?"

"Well, yeah . . . okay. I'll try. Thanks."

"Thank *you*, Phil. And let's keep up on the Yankees, okay? I don't see how they can lose this year, with Mantle hitting the way he is. And your cousin's off to a great start."

I grinned. "I know."

Two amazing things happened on the weekend of my ninth birthday, May 31, 1956. The first was the Indianapolis 500 Mile Race. As Dad had predicted, I saw far more people that May than I had ever seen before. It actually started when one guy nosed his truck up to a gate outside the track late in April. The same guy was the first to arrive every year, and no one ever knew exactly when he would show up. His appearance was welcomed as a sign of spring, like the swallows when they come back to Capistrano.

The racetrack itself opened for cars to practice on May 1. From that moment on, more and more people began pouring into town each day to watch the daily practice sessions and weekend time trials. It felt like Speedway was being inflated. Our neighbors were frantically clearing out space for their relatives and friends in spare rooms, basements, even garages. About every store in town had black-and-white checkered patterns on their awnings and in their windows. Racecar drivers' kids joined our classes at Fisher. And every day as I thumped my rubber ball against the garage after school, the whine of the engines a mile away grew louder.

At five P.M. on the day before the race, a great horn sounded throughout Speedway and the streets around the track were closed to traffic. Instantly cars, trucks, trailers, vans, and rigs of all description lined up behind the racetrack's gates. Within hours, the line on Sixteenth Street had backed up in two lanes across the White River and all the way into the middle of Indianapolis. Each vehicle was filled with fans waiting for the track's gates to open the next morning. Some cooked fried chicken and swigged beer from atop high platforms they had bolted on to their trucks. The scene became a colossal street carnival, complete with a midway across from the track. Midget races blazed all night. I walked with my parents down Crawfordsville Road and Sixteenth Street, clutching their hands tightly as we picked our way through the mob. Dances broke out and bonfires blazed. You could see license plates from everywhere.

The next day, we sat out back and grilled burgers and listened to the race in stereo. In one ear I could hear the drone of the cars through the radio, as a tag team of announcers followed the leaders around "the famed two-and-a-half-mile oval." For four hours the same four guys kept saying "over to you, Jack" *zooooom* "Over to you, Charlie" *zoooom*. And in the other ear I could hear the full-throated roar of the actual cars just down the road.

It was an exciting race. An amazing number of tires blew out, producing a litter of tire scraps all over the track, but somehow the drivers were usually able to gun their cars through the gauntlet. There were plenty of wrecks but no one got killed. While listening to the broadcast, I learned fabulous new vocabulary words. Drivers climbed into "Turbocharged Novis" and "Offenhausers" and got stalled with "magneto troubles." About three o'clock, the winner, Pat Flaherty, "took the checkered flag," drove a final leisurely victory lap, and then nosed his car into the pits to be surrounded by his crew. He climbed out of his car grinning, ducked under a wreath of flowers, and chugged down an entire bottle of milk as his wife and a beauty queen fussed over him. Minutes later, the first of a weary army of fans appeared on Speedway Drive, soon shuffling past our corner on their way to their cars and the long drive home. Their faces and arms were lobster-red from the sun. I stood on the corner and chatted with them as they filed by. That night, I thought about the drivers: They were brave and skilled, but they still didn't seem like real athletes to me. Basically they spent their afternoon making 800 or so left turns, unless they wrecked first. How hard was that, compared to hitting a moving baseball with a bat?

Speedway was a trash heap the next day, and the whole town seemed to have a hangover. But what did it matter to me? At last it was time for the real Memorial Day excitement—my birthday. Nine at last! After I tore through a few cards and gifts from my grandparents, and thanked my parents for a subscription to the *Sporting News,* I attacked the last square box, wrapped in plain brown paper and bundled in twine. From a soft lining of newspaper pages, I lifted a New York Yankee ball cap. Brownish stains discolored the sweatband. The bill was carefully fashioned into a smooth crescent. The N and the Y were intricately stitched with hundreds of small threads. It was a real Yankee cap—one that had been used in a game. Don Larsen had perspired in it, pulled its bill down over his eyes, wiped his brow with it—*and sent it to me*. This object had probably been sixty feet, six inches from Ted Williams, with the bill pointed right at him. Digging farther into the box, I pulled out a postcard wishing me good luck and a happy birthday. It was amazing and wonderful that he had done that for me.

I took the cap to school Monday morning, holding it out delicately in front of me as I walked up the stairs and into the room. Classmates gathered around as though I had brought in a new baby brother or sister. Then someone grabbed it and jammed it on his head. They passed it around as I lunged for it. Even a few girls tried it on, and then I snatched it back. The bill was bent. It made me sick. I felt my status being silently recalculated in the hostile silence.

"Won't make *you* play any better," one of them finally said.

I stood my ground. "You got a cousin on the Yankees?" I demanded.

"I don't *need* one," he replied.

CHAPTER FOUR

A LL RIGHT," I said. "One-two-*three!*" My best friend Herb Crawford and I flung open the door of my bedroom closet and recoiled in terror. Our eyes shot to the floor. There was nothing but the same old ripe-smelling pile of cleats, sneakers, and church shoes. From the safety of my bed I stirred them around with the knob end of my bat, teasing them apart carefully until bare floor tile was exposed. There were no pods to be seen. That made my whole bedroom pod-free. There had been none under the bed. None behind my chest of drawers. Together we let out a sigh of relief. Herb had slept over the night before. We had decided to watch one more TV movie before we went to sleep. It turned out to be *Invasion of the Body Snatchers*. We saw it mainly through our fingers.

It's a story about aliens from another planet who take over Earth by killing everyone and then copying them. They absorbed your personality, duplicated your mind, and then planted a replica of you in a seed pod that looked like a watermelon. The aliens were better people-copiers than pod-hiders, because all movie long, people kept stumbling into their own pods. One pod got discovered on a pool table—the unfinished humanoid actually opened its eyes and stared back at the real person. One woman got duplicated during a kiss. At the end, the hero staggers out onto a busy highway, waving his hands at the passing motorists, and screaming "You're next! You're next!" By the end, only a few real people were left, and the fate of the world depended on them.

There were a lot of movies like that in 1956, when we were on constant guard against the Russians, whom we knew as godless people who had the Bomb, were racing us in space, and were out to brainwash us until we couldn't think for ourselves any more. Another bunch of movies were about mutant creatures formed when A-bombs or H-bombs exploded or radioactive material escaped from a lab. The material oozed and seeped and glowed and sometimes grew limbs like ours and was always out to get us. Even in school, sometimes we had to watch a filmstrip instructing us to crawl under our desks and make like turtles in the event an atomic bomb exploded nearby. There was a lot to be afraid of back then.

Right before we turned the lights out, I had snuck a final glance at Herb out of the corner of my eye. He seemed to be glancing back at me out of the corner of his. He appeared to be the same: skinny, butch haircut, one eye that didn't quite track like the other. If the creature looking back at me wasn't the real Herb, the aliens had done a mighty good job. But the night had passed and now we were awake, and I was still me and Herb at least still acted like Herb. It was already warm out. We had wasted the whole morning looking for pods. Skipping breakfast, we spiked our gloves on our handlebars and took off for the Tenth Street diamond. One of the great things about Herb was that he liked to practice baseball as much as I did. Games were great, but we didn't need them. When there was nobody else to play with, we'd play endless two-person games: flies and grounders, step-back, pepper, hot box, burnout, modified versions of all of the above.

"Burnout" was the one I liked best. It was baseball's version of "blink." Two players paced off a distance, turned, and fired the ball back and forth at each other as hard as they could. First one to miss, or drop a ball, lost. Burnout played to my only strength. Baseball scouts rated players in terms of the five "tools," namely running, throwing, fielding, hitting, and hitting for power. Willie Mays was a five-tool player because he excelled in all these areas. Mickey Mantle was probably a 4.5, excelling at everything but fielding, since he occasionally didn't catch balls he couldn't out-run. I rated Herb about a 3.5. He did everything well except hit for power and throw. I was a half-tool man, rescued from total toollessness because I could throw hard. Admittedly, there was no way to know in which county any ball I threw would land, but how important was that? Don was wild too, and he was a Yankee.

Most of our burnout conversations ended up something like this:

Me: "I win! You missed!"

Herb: "It was uncatchable!"

Me: "Catchable!"

Herb: "Maybe by someone in Plainfield."

Me: "Go get it, loser . . ."

Herb: "He who throws, goes . . ."

Herb and I had both recently become Speedway Giants, one of the six teams in "D League," organized for the youngest ballplayers in Speedway. I had played so much by myself at the garage and with Dad out back in the spring that I entered the tryout as only one of the two or three worst players my age in town, rather than the worst in Speedway's history. Though I hungered to pitch, I tried out for second base, since only one other kid was going out for the position. I practiced by bouncing grounders to myself against the garage door. The soft rubber ball bounded back to me in true, regular hops. But at the tryout everything was different: The infield was rutted by spikes and littered with pebbles. Batted balls were on me before I could even react. I had no idea where they would go. After one glanced off my shoulder, I shied away from the rest.

Herb was a first baseman. He wasn't big, but he was slick, and no one messed with him because he was smarter than everyone else. He operated by his own rules, informed by his own logic. Once during the season when an opposing pitcher hit one of our batters, Herb trotted out of our dugout, grabbed the kid's glove right off his hand, and cut a notch in it with his pocketknife. The coaches were too stunned to do anything about it. The kid just looked down at his glove until the umpire called for play to resume. I loved Herb.

As a rule, I scorned uniforms of all kinds. There were photos around the house of my dad in his Navy blues and circular white sailor's hat, all reminders of the years he was torn away from us. To me, anyone in uniform—nurses, cops, insect exterminators, anyone—was a person not to be trusted. My philosophy was that if a person had real authority, like Mr. Northcott, they wouldn't have to wear a uniform. But on game day, the best day of the week, I was proud to don the green and white of the Speedway Giants.

A Giant built his uniform from the bottom up. First you hoisted green stirruped socks above the knee. Then you lowered your smartly pinstriped, cotton-white trouser legs over the sock, and tucked them back under themselves by about an inch. Then came the (regrettably) numberless green T-shirt with SPEEDWAY GIANTS emblazoned on the front, followed by rubber cleats, which turned out to leave black scuff marks on kitchen floor tile. Finally, the discriminating Giant turned to personal grooming. You slicked back your cowlick and spent a half hour or so in front of the mirror shaping the bill of your hat. Some kids put a bend in the middle, and others two bends in thirds. I opted for a continuous arc that distributed the stress of the bend equally along the bill surface.

Don Larsen's postcard was my model for bill-shaping. I propped it beside the mirror on game day. I got so I could perfectly imitate every aspect of the image. I had his followthrough down so beautifully that no one could have possibly known the difference between him and me in silhouette, unless they happened to notice his protruding ears or the stems of my glasses.

Last, but far from least, in my game-day ritual was glove prep. I had already owned two gloves in the six months we'd lived in Speedway. First had been the bright-orange clam Dad bought me from Sears on that day in March. We tried everything to loosen it up. Dad rubbed "neat's-foot oil" on it ("Dad, what's a 'neat'?"). I rolled it in a towel and slept on it. I put a ball in it and jumped on it. We slathered it with shaving cream and stuck it in the oven at 350 degrees for three minutes four times in a row, and all it did was change color. Kids at school swore by all sorts of methods. One said his dad drove their car back and forth over his glove. We weren't that dumb, but it wouldn't have mattered. A Sherman tank couldn't have broken in my glove. My glove was the hardest object on earth.

My second glove was the prize for selling the seventeenth-most marshmallows in my Cub Scout den. On the night of the award ceremony, I and each other young sales champion, dressed in full Cub uniform, bounded down the bleachers of the high school gym and pawed through the prizes on a table. The best thing left by the time I got there was a Franklin first-baseman's mitt, the only glove on the table. But I quickly fell out of love with it, since it proved even harder to use in fielding grounders than the Sears glove.

Then I met the Wilson A2000. I first saw it in the back of a *Baseball Digest*. There was Ted Williams, tanned, confident, smiling at me with gleaming white teeth. Formed around his right hand was the DeSoto of gloves. I was helpless. It was hard to say what I liked about it so much. The black-and-yellow tag was not nearly as pretty as the Rawlings crimson or the Spalding cobalt. Ted Williams wasn't really much of a fielder, and he was on the Red Sox to boot. But there was something about the A2000, maybe the color of the leather, perhaps its perfectly symmetrical shape, some perfection to the way it looked on Ted's hand.

Whatever it was, I fell blindly, overwhelmingly in love. I had to have it.

We had two sporting-goods stores on the west side of Indianapolis, Sports-Spot and Em-Roe. Both had the A2000 in stock, and salesmen at both stores would be only too happy to slip it on my hand for the rock-bottom 10 percent Speedway Little-League-discount price of $36.50. I did the numbers: I got a quarter-a-week allowance each Thursday morning and usually had it spent on baseball cards by noon. If I saved my allowance and didn't buy one pack of cards, I'd be able to buy my A2000 in 146 weeks—almost three years. I would be about to turn twelve. My parents chuckled when I pitched the A2000 as an investment in solid fielding, which would relieve stress and be good for the whole family. I next proposed we split the cost, with them fronting the money. Mom looked away. Dad reached for his pipe. My birthday had already passed, and it was nearly six months till Christmas. The conclusion was inescapable: I needed a job.

The *Speedway Flyer* was a free neighborhood paper that we picked out of the front bushes once a week. Delivery boys flung it at houses from their bicycles, speeding away too quickly for consequence. Delivering the *Flyer* was the only job available for someone my age. Mom and Dad agreed to let me apply, as long as I found a route in our neighborhood that wouldn't make me cross busy Sixteenth Street. So one day after school I pedaled up to a tin shack with a dozen or so bikes parked outside. I ducked inside and when my eyes adjusted, I saw a bunch of boys I knew rolling papers and stuffing them into saddlebags. A man sat at a desk in the corner, scribbling numbers on a form under a goose-necked lamp.

The nameplate said he was Mr. Ross. "I need a job," I said. He didn't look up. He was skinny, with pale skin drawn tight over jutting cheekbones. After a minute or two, I said louder, "I need a job." He pushed a piece of paper my way, told me to fill it out, and went back to his numbers.

A week later, he called. A route had opened up near my house. I rode down to the shack after school, and Mr. Ross stood up from his desk.

"You got a bike?"

"Yeah." He shoved a map of Speedway across his desktop.

"You know these streets?"

Winton. Cord. Auburn. It was my neighborhood.

"Sure."

His eyes narrowed. "Kid, there's one sure way to have a very short career here. That's to throw papers. We got a town full of Whitey Fords who think that any paper that lands inside Marion County is a strike. All those kids are in the minors now. Listen hard: You can either walk this route or ride it—your choice. But if you ride it, you get off your bike at every single house and place each paper neatly on the porch. You understand?"

"Yessir."

"You only get one strike here. One complaint about a paper in the bushes, and you're out."

"Yessir."

"Roll your papers over there. You get two bucks a week. Pick it up here after you finish your route."

Two dollars a week!!! I did the math. It meant I'd have the A2000 by Christmas. I thanked him and started rolling papers.

As I vaulted onto my bike, I was thinking, "What a break . . . here is the job I was made for. It'll strengthen my arm and improve my eye. Who could miss a whole front porch from the sidewalk?" I reached back and withdrew a tightly rolled *Flyer* from the canvas sack behind me, slowing as I pedaled toward the first house at the corner of Speedway Drive and Winton. Taking steady aim, I rifled the paper end-over-end into Jerry Crane's dad's roof gutter. An instant later I saw Mr. Crane working on his shrubs. Mr. Crane was a Sunday school teacher who barely spoke above a whisper in class. I took off. He screamed at me, "Phil Hoose! You stop right now!!" Fool that I was, I did. I begged him not to call Mr. Ross, and after I climbed up on his stepladder and dropped the paper down to him, he didn't. I walked the route from then on, dreaming step by step of the winter day when I would finally slip my Wilson A2000 over my left wrist.

Since the Giant coaching staff had to put me somewhere, they made me an outfielder. I might have sulked the whole summer about not getting a chance to pitch—my ultimate ambition, even though I had tried out for second—had not one of our coaches, Mr. Harley, taken me on as a project. He didn't seem to mind that I wasn't as strong or experienced as the others, but it drove him berserk if I didn't concentrate. "You can't just scratch your butt out there between pitches, Phil," he'd say. "Think!"

"About what?"

"About what?? . . . About what you're gonna do if the ball is hit to you, that's what! What if it comes on the ground? What if it's in the air? What if it's over your head? In front of you? What if there are two out? One? Runners on first and third? A runner on second? Who you gonna throw it to?"

I became Mr. Harley's Irish setter. He hit hundreds of balls to me, mainly because I never got tired of chasing them. He could slice it just out of my reach in any direction, until, very gradually, I began to get the hang of it. I got so I could predict how far the ball would travel by the sound it made when it hit his bat. He taught me to kneel down and block one-hoppers with my whole body rather than just swiping at the ball with my glove as it skipped by. I learned to run in on an easy fly ball before a long throw to the infield so I could apply the momentum of my entire body to the throw. Thin, heavy-bearded, and soft-spoken, Mr. Harley nipped bad habits before I could form them. "Never backpedal when a ball's hit over your head, Phil," he'd say. "Turn around and run to the spot where the ball is going be."

"How will I know?"

"That's what we're here for."

During these practices, a strange thing started to happen. I fell in love with baseball. At first, this game had been a chore, something I had to learn in order to stay afloat with the boys at school. There had been little joy in throwing a rubber ball against the garage in the early spring darkness. But as I played with others in the long, warm evenings of June, I began to take pleasure in the game. You had to be brave to play baseball, but you didn't have to be especially tough. The point wasn't to slam into each other. Baseball was not about marching down a field or scoring a certain number of points before time ran out; in fact, theoretically a baseball game could last forever. I loved the pause at the end of every pitch and every out that gave you a chance to rub dirt on your hands or look up at the clouds. I wasn't tough, and I didn't especially want to be. My favorite book not written by John R. Tunis was *Ferdinand,* about a bull who would rather daydream beneath a cork tree than battle a matador. That was me.

However, a wandering mind was the outfielder's worst enemy. Infielders and pitchers were right up close to the action, balanced forward in tiptoe stances, pounding their gloves and chattering and spitting and squinting and thinking two steps ahead. Far behind them, I stood straight up picking my seat. Late afternoon clouds twisted up into dragons and sharks. The sun felt nice on my back. Was that a four-leaf clover? Who were the Yankees playing tonight? Was Don pitching? Why wouldn't Mr. Harley let me pitch?

The one play I dreaded above all others was the Texas Leaguer. When a ball was looped over the infield and into the shallow part of the outfield, I was supposed to sprint in toward the diamond as fast as I could and try to make the lunging catch at my shoe-tops. My thick glasses bounced on the bridge of my nose with every step, and with them my vision of the ball. Those glasses, and the mole-weak eyes behind them, were my biggest problem as a ballplayer.

I had first realized how nearsighted I was one winter evening when we pulled the Plymouth up to Rosner's Drugs in downtown Speedway and Dad went inside to get pipe cleaners. As we waited, Mom said something about the IMPEACH EARL WARREN sign across Sixteenth Street from the race track.

"Where?" I asked.

"What do you mean, 'where'?"

"Where's the sign that says IMPEACH EARL WARREN?"

A week later, I was in the office of Dr. Richard Tubesing, Speedway's only optometrist. He was a chunky, talkative man with a burr haircut. The odor of stale smoke clung to his white lab coat. Whenever he scooted forward in his chair to blast a puff of air into my eyeball or blind me with a small flashlight, my nose got pushed close to the pack of Viceroys bulging in his pocket. When I had to follow his finger to the left, my eyes encountered the bill of a giant sailfish mounted on his office wall, a blue-green monster that must have scared the bubbles out of anything that came near it. Its arched back glittered like a rainbow, and its lance-like bill had surely shredded many an enemy into a meal. It seemed sad that a great warrior fish would end up on an optometrist's wall in Indiana. Through his Viceroy-rich breath, Dr. Tubesing asked me the same four questions every time.

"How many fingers?"

"Which is clearer, one, or two?"

"When do the letters line up?"

"Which is clearer: the green half, or the red?"

Like everyone else in town, Dr. Tubesing gave me homework. His was a series of cards filled with rows of figures. In addition to not recognizing objects far away, my eyes didn't focus properly. My job was to make the figures converge.

It was just one more set of muscles to strengthen, and I worked hard at it. I had to see, because I couldn't hit. I was improving as an outfielder, and my arm was getting stronger by the day, but a

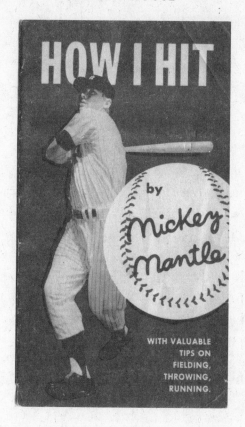

pitched ball came in too fast for me to see very well, and I was terrified of getting struck by the ball.

My bible for batting was a small, maroon-colored pamphlet entitled *How I Hit,* by Mickey Mantle. It came with a bar of Lifebuoy Soap that Mom had brought home. Page one was "My Batting Secret," in which Mantle revealed that "Good hitters are *not* born: they are made." Music to my ears. Mick also said that "it's not how much power you *have* but how much power you *use*." Again, this was great news, because I was very short on power.

Mickey Mantle was my god. He was the strongest, fastest, most-feared, and best-looking player in baseball. The year before, he had led the American league in homers, extra-base hits, walks, on-base percentage, slugging percentage, and triples. They said he ran so fast that he could make it from home to first base in 3.1 seconds when he batted left-handed. Several times a day, I counted out three seconds on the classroom clock and tried to imagine Mantle running to first. It seemed impossible. Twice, Mickey Mantle almost hit balls completely out of Yankee Stadium. It was an incredible distance. Even his routine homers were said to have been "blasted." They clanged off light towers and dented steel supports and cleared boulevards, finally coming to rest in startled peoples' backyards.

Mickey Mantle improved my vocabulary by introducing me to such words as "filigree" and "façade." These were architectural features of Yankee Stadium that he alone occasionally struck or even cleared with monstrous shots, sending Yankee publicists with tape measures scrambling after the bounding balls. Mickey Mantle was like a comic-book hero, employing the structures of the city to demonstrate his mighty strength. Once, in a game Don pitched in June, Mantle hit a ball on top of the roof of Detroit's Briggs Stadium. It bounced onto Trumbull Avenue, where a man ran it down, leaped into his car, and took off with it. When he got home, he telephoned the Tigers and said he'd return it the next day, but only if he got a chance to give it to Mantle himself.

Mickey Mantle was more famous than anyone except Elvis and Marilyn Monroe and maybe President Eisenhower.

My favorite thought was that the Mick spent part of every day with my cousin. I liked to imagine them ribbing each other, talking baseball, pointing out starlets and stewardesses from the dugout. I imagined that sometimes in the quiet of a hotel bar in Kansas City or Cleveland, Don and Mickey talked about me. I made up the conversations in my head, since I couldn't be there:

"Hey, Don, how's Darwin's boy doing?"

"Phil?"

"Yeah, Phil, out in Indiana. How's he coming with his baseball?"

"Mick, it's gotta be tough for him. He's just starting out. But one thing I love about the kid . . . he never quits. When he sets his mind to something, you can bet he'll do it or die trying."

"Sounds like a great kid, Don. Reminds me of myself when I was his age."

At night I took my bat inside our bathroom and locked the door, imitating Mantle's stance in the full-length mirror until I had it down perfectly. My front foot was exactly fifteen inches behind the piece of cardboard I had cut into the shape of home plate and placed on the floor. My toe, like Mick's toe, was right in line with the plate's edge. I was the perfect imitation of the game's greatest power hitter.

But in a game it was different. When a real pitch zoomed toward me, appearing as a deadly little white seed through my thick glasses, my front foot led my entire body in full-scale retreat. In one of my library books, Ty Cobb said, "Every great batter works on the theory that the pitcher is more afraid of him than

Me imitating Mickey Mantle's stance in Speedway

he is of the pitcher." That was the difference between Ty and me. I would rather go to the dentist than bat against Buzz Benedetto or Butch Matthews. It didn't help when I saw one kid get hit in the eye by a pitch he couldn't dodge fast enough. The ball made a small clicking sound against his face. All summer long, my coaches screamed at me through cupped hands, "Get your foot out of the *bucket,* Hoose!!" "Putting your foot in the bucket" was ancient baseball lingo for stepping away from a pitch. I heard them yelling, but the click of the ball against bone was even louder.

Mickey Mantle didn't say anything about fear in *How I Hit,* but he did share his rules for living. Mick lined them out in neat categories:

Diet: "Always eat some of everything on your plate. Don't neglect fresh fruit, vegetables and salads."

Sleep: "When I was your age, I always tried to get at least 9 or 10 hours of sleep a night. You'll find your reflexes are a lot sharper when you're not all tired out from being up too late!" (This seemed strange, because the Mick was often written about as a guy who stayed up pretty late, like my cousin Don. But night-owling must have been working for both of them, since the Yanks were running away from everyone else in the league throughout the summer, and they were both having great seasons.)

Cleanliness: "After every game—and once a day every day—I always take a bath or shower with my favorite soap, Lifebuoy. That's because I've learned that staying clean is a big part of staying in condition. Lifebuoy not only gets you clean, it helps keep germs away. It has a special germ fighter in it called TMTD.

Lifebuoy ad in Mickey Mantle's pamphlet *How I Hit*

Most of my big-league friends like Lifebuoy. I hope you will too!" I wondered if Mick ever loaned Don a bar of Lifebuoy when they showered together. I made a note to ask him.

"Hoose, hit for Hubbell!"

Mr. Harley's words jolted me out of my dugout daydream one afternoon during a game and sent me scurrying toward the bat rack.

I pulled out a bat, jammed on a helmet, pretended to knock the dirt off my cleats with my bat (not that there was any dirt on them, since I hadn't been out of the dugout all game), and stepped into the batter's box. Pushing my glasses up my nose, I blinked out at Buzz Benedetto. He was leering back at me. "What a break," his expression said. "Hoose. Automatic out."

"Hoose, put the trademark up!" Mr. Harley hollered from the dugout. That was nice of him to say, especially loud enough for everyone else to hear. It was well known that a bat was more likely to shatter upon impact with a pitched ball if the Louisville Slugger trademark burned into the bat barrel wasn't held up so the batter could see it. Mr. Harley was publicly pretending that I was about to endanger a piece of our team's equipment by hitting a pitch with it.

There was one out and a runner on first. We Giants were behind 6–3 in the fifth. As I raised my bat in a perfect imitation of Mantle, four infielders crept toward me as if I were certain to bunt. The outfielders edged in closer too, nearly to the back edge of the infield. Who could blame them? Everyone in the league

knew I hadn't hit a ball fair all summer. It would have been insane to play me like a real batter.

At such close range, I could hear them all chattering, even the
outfielders.

"Heybatterbatterbatterbatter"

"NobatterinthereBuzz"

"ChuckhardBuzz"

"You the man, Buzz"

"Comebabefirehard . . . youthemanBuzz"

"Buzzbuzzbuzzbuzzbuzzbuzz"

Buzz Benedetto spat, set himself, peeked back over his left
shoulder at the runner on first, glared at me, and fired the ball
sidearm. I could hear it whizzing toward me. I pulled my front
leg away from the ball as usual, but for the first time the rest of
my body lunged forward, allowing me to flick the bat in a tight
arc out over the plate. I felt a shock in my hands, heard a sharp
crack, and saw the ball bounding rapidly toward the shortstop. I
stood at the plate, watching. The fielder picked it up, flipped it to
the second basemen who touched the base, and lobbed it over to
first. Double play.

"Why didn't you *run,* Hoose?" yelled Mr. Harley, hands outstretched. My teammates disgustedly picked up their gloves and
trotted muttering out into the field. I was still standing there in
the box, a smile broadening into a grin. I hit it. *I hit it.* I finally,
finally hit it. I passed Herb at first base on my way out to right
field, where Mr. Harley told me to play. He was grinning
too, and had a hand outstretched for me to slap on the way by.
"Way to go, man. You didn't look scared either!" After the game,

Mr. Harley draped his hand over my shoulder. "Sorry I yelled at you, Phil. Come early for practice Wednesday and I'll pitch to you extra. Now we have something to build on."

I stayed awake all that night. I kept hearing that crack over and over, and seeing the ball shoot fast out in front of me, not dribbling but bounding, propelled by the force of my swing. At last Mantle and I had something in common besides the soap we used. We had both hit fair balls in a baseball game. True, I didn't "blast" my two-hopper to shortstop. It didn't bang off any buildings or carom off any steel supports or clear a filigree or "come to rest" in anyone's yard. No publicist went scrambling after it with a tape measure to see how far it went. But I could feel it—my days as an automatic out were numbered.

CHAPTER FIVE

THE SUMMER DAYS were as long now as they would ever be. Locusts sang from maple leaves in the backyard until bedtime. Slabs of beef sizzled and popped on backyard grills. Little kids with empty Mason jars chased lightning bugs around the tiny backyards on our block while grown-ups just sat talking and talking, pausing only to pick pieces of corn from their teeth. On nights when we Speedway Giants didn't have games, I stayed out in the driveway until late, winding up, setting, checking the runners, and whipping my rubber ball against the garage door. Bang. Bang. *Bang.* The sound was getting louder now. Cinders could rarely catch up to the ball when it bounded back to me.

One night I got called in early for dinner, right after Dad got home from work. I retired the final batter, accepted the congratulations of my teammates, and walked inside, letting the screen door slam behind me. I splashed water on my hands and sat down to meat loaf and a baked potato. An envelope was sticking out from beneath my plate. "What's this?" I asked my parents. "Only one way to find out," my dad said. I ripped it open. Inside was a ticket. "Chicago White Sox vs. New York Yankees." The date was a month away.

They were both watching me. I looked up. "Is this for real?" I asked. "Sure is," said my mom, smiling now. "Don set aside three tickets for us. He promised to meet us after the game."

This was unimaginable. I was going to see the Yankees. I was going to meet my cousin. I was going to watch Mickey Mantle in person. I suddenly felt an overwhelming need for information about the Yanks, almost as if I were cramming for a test. I had to know more about Mantle's ongoing quest to break Babe Ruth's single-season home run record, about Don Larsen's game-by-game fortunes. I turned to three sources of information: the radio, the *Sporting News,* and the *Indianapolis Star.* Of these, the radio was by far the most important.

Packed in a Bible-sized, felt-lined case, my transistor radio looked like a toy, and in fact had been a Christmas gift, but when I was alone in my room this small object brought the baseball universe into my ear. Each night when the summer light died, I leaped into bed. Racing through my prayers (Bless my family, bless all those less fortunate than me, bless the Yanks), I kissed my parents good-night and lay stiff until the door clicked shut. Then I fumbled under my mattress for the radio's earplug and jammed it into my ear. No one else could hear the radio as long as I used the plug. Alone at last, I went game-casting. Often I fell asleep with the plug in my ear.

On clear summer nights, the whole Midwest turned into a ballfield. Night after night, a handful of powerful, clear-channel,

50,000-watt radio stations transmitted games from the tops of their mighty towers out over the flat fields and little towns. I lay under an invisible web of radio beams. With no mountains to obstruct them, the Cardinals, Cubs, White Sox, Reds, and Indians sailed into my bedroom on clouds of smoke and sudsy oceans of beer.

The Cardinals came all the way from the Mississippi River on the very same station, KMOX, that had delivered them to Grandpa Brown and Uncle Tom in Carbon decades before. Their announcers, Jack Buck and Harry Caray, were the best anywhere. From WCFL in Chicago, General Cigar brought me the voices of Bob Elson and Don Wells and the Chicago White Sox. From Crosley Field in Cincinnati, "Burger, the Beer that Brings You Baseball!" delivered the Cincinnati Reds, featuring sleeveless slugger Ted Kluszewski and rookie phenom Frank Robinson.

I listened intently for Yankee scores. Whenever announcers from American League teams gave the scores of other games being played that night, they read the other American League scores first, paused for a beat and said "over in the National League," before reciting the NL scores, and vice-versa. They made it seem as if the American and National leagues were separate universes, hemispheres that came together under tightly controlled circumstances only during the All-Star Game and the World Series.

To me the most obvious difference between the two leagues was that almost all the good Negro players played over in the National League. Willie Mays, Ernie Banks, Roberto Clemente,

Jackie Robinson, Henry Aaron, Roy Campanella, Don Newcombe, and now, Frank Robinson—all the great black players
were over there. The American League didn't have a single black
star in 1956, unless you counted Cuban-born Minnie Minoso—
and there were very few Negro players period in the Junior Circuit. The Red Sox and Tigers had no blacks at all, and the
Yankees only one—Elston Howard, a catcher who backed up
Yogi Berra and played the outfield.

The two leagues were a lot like Speedway and Indianapolis to
me. Our two cities were physically connected—if you stood on
the west side of the Sixteenth Street bridge you were in Speedway, on the east side in Indianapolis—but Speedway held itself
stiffly apart from "Indianoplace." In baseball terms, Speedway
was definitely an American League town. We only had one Negro family, the Burtons, among our twelve thousand residents.
Evelyn Burton was in my grade at school. Tall and shy, she was
the only dark-skinned person I had ever been even remotely
near. I had never worked up the nerve to speak to her.

Indianapolis was our National League. When Dad drove us
into the city, as we approached the White River we always passed
through a neighborhood almost all of whose residents were
black. Through the back window of our Plymouth I could see
black kids running and playing, or just sitting on porches with
their families and friends. Every now and then they looked back
at me as we drove by. I wondered if their lives were anything like
mine.

Sometimes, as we pedaled home from the Tenth Street diamond, Herb and I would ask each other, "Is there any Negro in

the world you'd trade places with?" Here was a question that could keep us absorbed for a long time. On one hand, anyone meant *anyone:* Johnny Mathis, Chuck Berry, Willie Mays, Martin Luther King. You could be a ballplayer or an actor or a musician. On the other hand, you'd have problems, and we didn't know what they'd feel like. You'd probably get put down by whites, who would outnumber you. There would be some places you couldn't go. We heard that there was only one day a year when Negroes could get into Riverside Amusement Park—arguably the best place in Indianapolis. That was "Polk Milk Day," when the park would admit black kids who brought in a certain number of bottle caps from a local dairy. Or maybe you'd feel totally invisible. My crayon box contained a peach-colored crayon named "flesh," which made it seem like that was the color of all human skin. In the cartoon stories on the backs of my baseball cards, black players were often drawn as whites with burr haircuts. But on the other hand, in our question, you could be anybody. Herb and I chewed this over, going back and forth. "So, is there anyone you would trade with?" Herb favored musicians like Chuck Berry. I said maybe Elston Howard.

Each night as I turned my radio dial in the darkness of my room, I kept searching for the Yankees. Unfortunately, it was almost impossible to get them. A hundred times or so a night I moved the needle back and forth over 1010, WINS in New York City. WABC in New York was pretty easy to get, but not WINS. I constantly adjusted my earplug and strained for the voice of Mel Allen or Red Barber, hoping they would whisper to me through the static. That whole summer, I heard them three times, each time on a clear, starry night. Once I heard Mantle hit what Mel Allen described as a "Ballantine Blast."

For daily news of the Yankees, I turned to the morning's *Indianapolis Star*. The accounts were brief and the language boring, but at least I could see whether Don pitched or Mantle blasted a homer. To nourish my soul, I subscribed to the *Sporting News,* a weekly paper out of St. Louis. The postman brought it every Friday. In this, the "Baseball Bible," you got not only a week's worth of major-league box scores but also scores and brief accounts from games at nine minor-league levels. You got the Northwest League, the Pioneer League and the All-Florida League, the Nebraska State League, the Sally League and the Three-I League. You even got the Mexican League. I read them all.

The *Sporting News* put the dust of a game right in your nostrils. Pitchers didn't pitch games, not in the *Sporting News*. Instead, they "twirled mound gems." Runs produced by errors were "tainted tallies." The first game of a doubleheader was the "lidlifter" and the second the "nightcap." Nobody ever hit a home run in the *Sporting News:* Circuit clouts and four-baggers were smashed, blasted, walloped, and belted. Batters whiffed when pitchers kayoed them. Pitchers who had their best stuff whitewashed opponents, often because infielders turned in twin killings, snagged blue darters, and snared frozen ropes. When pitchers faltered, it was usually because their control deserted them, at which point they began to issue free passes. Teams hammered, zeroed, drubbed, pasted, and nipped each other. As much as I wanted to clout four-baggers and twirl gems of my own some day, I wanted to grow up to write like that even more. I longed to paint pictures with words some day.

We left early in the morning, with a car full of packed lunches, so that I could get to Chicago in time to see Mantle take batting practice. I sat alone in the backseat as always, reading steadily from my rapidly growing personal baseball library. I brought along several John R. Tunises, several issues of *Baseball Digest* and the *Sporting News,* along with *The Official Encyclopedia of Baseball* (Revised Edition), several player biographies, and my autograph book. A few miles out of Speedway, as green rows of corn blurred by on both sides of US 52, I absorbed myself in an article about the 1946 World Series. When I got to the part about Enos Slaughter scoring from first on a single, I stumbled over a sentence that read, "Slide, you bastard, slide!" As always, I asked about any word I hadn't seen before.

"Mom, what's a bastard?" The car swerved sharply.

"What are you *reading*?" my mom demanded.

"*Baseball Digest*." I held up the cover.

"That's not a word for you to worry about, Phil."

"Okay," I said, making a note to look it up as soon as I got home.

The farm towns rushed by in a regular pattern: cornfields, the Lion's Club sign, a gas station, three or four blocks of houses and stores, the town square surrounding a Civil War statue, three or four more blocks of houses and stores, a cemetery, the back of the other Lion's Club sign, and more cornfields. Whenever we'd pass a cemetery, Mom would point out the window and crack her immortal joke:

"How many people are dead there?"

Dad and I would roll our eyes. "I don't know."

"All of them," she'd cackle.

The clouds began to thicken near Lafayette—our halfway point. I looked out the back as sprinkles plopped on the Plymouth fins and beaded up on the trunk. The sky was an angry purple as we neared Gary. It was pouring when we reached Chicago.

The Yankee–White Sox game was rained out. I stopped crying only after my dad sprinted back from a phone booth, my copy of the *Sporting News* covering his head, to tell us that we were going to meet Don at Chicago's Del Prado Hotel, where the Yankees were staying. We pulled up into the lot and ran through the downpour and in and around the revolving door, and there he was, waiting for us.

Don Larsen was by far the biggest human being I had ever seen. He wore a loose-fitting brown suit with pants whose creases seemed to converge somewhere over my head. After he greeted my dad with a firm handshake and my mom with a warm smile, he looked down at me. I offered him my hand. Instead, he wrapped his arms around me and pulled my head into his stomach. He seemed glad to see me. He asked me if I would like to meet a few of the Yankees. I could barely answer him.

The New York Yankees were easy to spot: They were the young men scattered about the hotel lobby wearing suits and ties and shiny shoes. They looked as if they had just come back from church and they were waiting around for something to happen. They looked strange without billed caps—I had never thought of them as having hair. Don took me around and introduced me. Johnny Kucks, a pitcher nearly as tall as Don, also gave me a hug. Whitey Ford bent down to my level and asked me what position I played. "Well, I want to be a pitcher," I stammered. He told me not to try to throw a curve too soon.

"Why not?"

"You're not ready. It'll hurt your arm."

"When will I be ready?"

"Later," he said, as someone else claimed his attention.

Don spotted Yankee manager Casey Stengel entertaining a cluster of baseball writers in the corner of the lobby. Don walked me toward him. "Go over there by yourself," he whispered, pushing me forward. "Go on . . . tell Casey you're my cousin." I walked a few paces, heart hammering, and waited until the wrinkled old man with enormous ears got to the punch line of his story.

When the laughter died down, I stepped in front of him and introduced myself. His eyes widened. "You're Larsen's cousin, eh?" I nodded. The skipper grabbed my arm and pulled me close to his side. "Well, Larsen's a good man, no matter what you read." Reporters chuckled. I felt embarrassed, like a prop. The sportswriters were enjoying this. I had only wanted to meet Stengel, not be in a play. I said the only thing I could think of. "I just finished reading your biography, Mr. Stengel." He broke up laughing, as if this was the funniest thing he had ever heard. "Lies, all lies!" he cackled. "Written by guys like these." Now they were laughing hard. Still clutching me, Casey Stengel swept his free arm around the little knot of reporters. "Take a good look at these faces, son," he said. "Look at 'em hard. Now let me give you one piece of advice. Whatever you do, don't grow up to be a writer."

Before I made it back to Don, who was talking to my parents, I spotted Mickey Mantle standing by himself at the cigar stand, flipping through a magazine. His head looked the same as it always did in the pictures, with a short blond crew cut, but his body looked different. He was shorter than I imagined—in fact, most of the Yankees were taller than he—but something about him was huge. It was his back, mainly, that made his suit coat bulge like that.

I started toward him, but Don spotted me first. He took my autograph book and said, "Wait here." Mantle signed it without looking up from his magazine and handed it back to Don. Deeply disappointed, I asked Don why I couldn't speak to him, and Larsen said so many people bothered Mantle that it was sort of an unwritten rule on the Yankees to protect his privacy. Don said I could watch him for a while if I didn't bother him. So I stood there out of sight, inspecting the man, trying to figure out what made him so great. You sure couldn't tell by the way he read a magazine.

Mom, Dad, Don, and I sat down for lunch in the hotel restaurant. While I was eating, somebody rubbed my head from behind. I turned around and looked up. It was Yogi Berra. He joined us for a few minutes and asked about my baseball life. All this seemed as if it were a dream, like it was happening to someone else, or not happening at all. For so long I had been told that Don Larsen was my cousin, and that I had this special relationship with the New York Yankees, but in a way until now I hadn't really believed it. Of course it was true, because my parents said it was true, but it still hadn't seemed real. There had always been a slim mathematical chance that they had made the whole thing up to make me feel better. Now there was no denying it. Don Larsen and Yogi Berra were at my table. New York Yankees were standing and sitting all around me, some of them greeting Don as "Froggie" or "Gooney." I was lunching with the best baseball players in the world.

We stayed overnight in Chicago and then headed for Comiskey Park in the morning to take in the next game in the series. The rain had moved out and the air was fresh and clean. Arriving two hours early so I could watch batting practice, we reported to the WILL CALL window, where golden people like us with special connections picked up their tickets. Shuffling through turnstiles, we passed into the dark innards of the stadium, where my nostrils exploded with the glory of hot dogs and cigar smoke. We paused to buy a scorecard, found our aisle number, and started up a ramp toward an ever-widening rectangle of brilliant sunlight. I came out of the tunnel, blinked back the light, and stopped.

I was standing in a colossal bowl, looking out at a vast, colorful scene. Thousands and thousands of freshly painted wooden seats gleamed bright up close in the sunlight, giving way to forest colors in the distant shadowy stands. Before me, men with garden hoses were spraying water on the blond infield dirt, turning it instantly to a rich chocolate. A young man pushed a machine on wheels to lay down a perfectly straight stripe of white lime between home plate and third. Freshly clipped outfield grass shone bright emerald. Along the stadium rooftop, the wind stiffened a group of eight evenly spaced pennants, one for each American League team. Far away, the iron-columned stands in left and right field converged upon a tall scoreboard in center field. Above all this was a hard blue sky. It was so beautiful, I felt like crying.

An usher let me walk down behind the Yankee dugout. A cage was soon rolled out and the Yanks, in gray road uniforms, started taking batting practice. Pitchers jogged lazily in groups of three

Comiskey Park circa 1956

and four along the outfield wall, chatting all the way. I saw Don's big number 18 in one quartet. A coach was hitting sky-high popups to the catchers with a long skinny bat. Knots of four or five batters took their turns, each taking a few swings and then jumping out of the cage. There was number 14, Skowron. Number 9, Bauer. Yogi, number 8. They were casual, chatty, confident; men who suddenly looked right with caps on their heads and numbers on their backs.

Mickey Mantle stood there waiting his turn, leaning on his bat and taking in the sun, the number 7 stretched tight across his wide back. He watched as others batted, then stepped in. The batting practice pitcher threw, and Mantle uncoiled. When his bat met the ball, it sounded like the crack of a rifle. The ball sped through the air in a long arc and crashed against the empty seats far away. He took several swings right-handed and several left-handed. Once he hit the ball completely out of the stadium.

No wonder the writers said he "blasted" balls. There was no better word. Nothing I could practice in the bathroom mirror would ever make that happen. How, I wondered, had he become that strong? Whatever it was, I was sure it had nothing to do with eating vegetables or TMTD or getting a good night's sleep. Mickey Mantle seemed like he belonged to a different species. After watching batting practice, I felt certain that no two human beings could possibly be more different than Mickey Mantle and me.

After the game, which the Yankees lost, we waited for Don at the players' gate. Cops struggled to hold back the mob, consisting mostly of kids clutching something to sign and looking for Mantle. The team bus waited at the curb, door open and motor running. Yankee players came out, one by one, dressed in suits again. Most chatted a little with the crowd, and those who stopped to sign were immediately engulfed by fans. Don came out, ever huge, spotted us, and came over to say good-bye. He asked the fans to give us a little room so my parents could take pictures of

Don and me outside Comiskey Park

My dad, Don, and me

Don and me against the red brick of Comiskey Park. Kids gawked. I was glad Mom had made me dress up. Right then, Mantle came out, head down, and started for the bus. Kids spilled past the cops to surround him. Mantle wordlessly bulled his way through the crowd. He kept his hands in his pants pockets and never looked up, his thick body brushing aside yearbooks and scorecards and autograph books thrust out for him to sign. He entered the bus without speaking or waving or looking back. I actually felt sorry for him. He didn't look like he was having any fun at all being Mickey Mantle. Don gave me a hug and said warm good-byes to Mom and Dad and made his way to the bus.

I slept all the way home. There would be stories for Herb and the other Giants, and for anyone else I could get to listen, but there would never be a way to describe what this weekend in Chicago had felt like or meant. By a margin of nine or ten games, these had been the best two days of my life.

CHAPTER SIX

AUGUST 1956
FROM THE *SPORTING NEWS:*
(SUNDAY AUGUST 12 (DAY); AT NEW YORK)

Mantle hit forty-first homer of season to move 13 games ahead of Ruth's record pace, as Yankees swept pair from Orioles, 6–2 and 4–2. Larsen hurled six-hitter and had more than enough support to rack up seventh victory in lidlifter.

A FTER HAVING MET the Yankees, I daydreamed about them constantly. We were always together, the players, the coaches, the Old Man, and me. I had a direct telepathic line to them on the field, in the dugout, even in the shower. In my imagination, each of them took an active interest in the shape of my career, and each had definite and stubbornly held opinions about how I should be coached. Sometimes this led to conflict, as in one post-game scene from Yankee Stadium. It started with an idle question from Mickey Mantle, addressed to Don:

"Hey, Gooney, how's Darwin's boy doing?"

Mantle had to shout to be heard above the hiss of the showers in the locker room. His mighty back glistened with TMTD, and bubbles of the great germ-fighting agent beaded in his crew cut. Like everyone else on the Yankees, Mantle called Don "Gooney Bird" or just "Gooney." This was because Don loved comic books and made no secret of it. He kept hundreds of them in his locker, and even ran a lending library. Any Yankee wishing to borrow a comic had to first deposit a dime in a tin cup Don kept by the locker. He enjoyed sharing the adventures he read with his teammates.

"What's that, Mick?"

"Phil. Darwin's boy. How's he doin'?" At the sound of my name, Whitey Ford placed his bar of Lifebuoy on the soap dish and splashed over to hear better.

"I just got a letter from him. He says they're gonna let him pitch." Larsen grinned. "He wants to be like me."

Mantle grinned back. "Great idea. A comic-book junkie who turns in about the time Phil wakes up. Some model you are." Then Mantle's brow furrowed, and a bubble of soap slid into his eye, causing him to wince, just like he did when his osteomyelitis acted up. "Why're they letting him pitch? I thought he just started playin'."

"I know. I'm a little worried about it too. He didn't look that big when we saw him in Chicago."

Ford interjected. "I did what I could, Mick. I warned him not to throw the curve too soon. He was already asking me about it."

Mantle stepped out from beneath the spray and faced the two pitchers. "What's this stuff about Chicago? Did you see him?"

"Yeah," said Larsen. "You coulda seen him too, if you'd looked up."

"What's that supposed to mean?"

"Phil's family came to see a game in Chicago last month. When we got rained out, he hung out with us in the hotel lobby." Ford nodded as Larsen, now growing uncomfortable, continued. "He saw you reading a magazine at the cigar stand and tried to get to you, but I headed him off, just like you told us to."

Now Mantle's hazel eyes turned serious. His level stare penetrated the slender curtain of drizzle into which the mammoth Larsen had retreated.

"Listen, Gooney Bird, if that boy ever shows up again, you bring him to me, hear? He may not be big, and his dad may not be teaching him like mine taught me, but he loves our game just like I loved it. I can tell. We're a lot alike, me and Phil."

"You're right, Mick. Okay. I'll try to get you a chance to meet him."

"I'd appreciate that, Gooney." And with that, Mantle retreated into his legendary sulk and resumed slowly coating the last muscles not already covered with Lifebuoy.

The last thing the Speedway Giants needed, Mr. Harley kept telling me, was an untested pitcher. "We already *have* Hubbell and Craig," he would say. "And even with them it doesn't look like we're gonna make the playoffs."

"So what do we have to lose?"

I pulled off my glasses and squinted up at him from under the bill of my green cap, hands on my hips. I knew what he was thinking, and he knew I knew, but he was too good a guy to say it. I needed more time before I got put in the line of fire. I still couldn't consistently field a grounder. I still sometimes threw to the wrong base after I caught an outfield fly, and my throws were disturbingly off-target no matter what my intent. I remained oh-for-the-season at the plate, and, though I sometimes hit the ball now, my front foot remained lodged in the bucket. In short, I was what veteran baseball scouts called a "project," made nearly uncoachable by my wild desire to learn everything at once. Of course it made no sense to Mr. Harley to put me in the line of fire. "We'll stay in the outfield this year, Phil," he would say gently, and try to change the subject.

That's what *he* thought. I was hell-bent-for-leather (a phrase used about once a page in *Baseball Digest*) to get my chance, and this year. I experienced life as a pitcher. The world was my mound. I hurled everywhere, in all settings. At Kroger's, Mom would send me to pick up some pork chops; but before I could get there, the bullpen phone would ring and I'd be told to heat up. A half hour later, Mom would come upon me in produce, leaning in to get the sign, shaking off my catcher, stepping off to get some resin, looking back in, checking the runners, winding, setting, and dealing. I pitched at the bus stop, and by the street crossing where I was supposed to be a traffic guard. I logged hundreds of innings in restrooms that had mirrors.

I pitched to Dad and to Herb and to anyone who would, or could, catch me. My arm was strengthening, but I was wild, like Don. With no one willing to teach me how to pitch, I imitated the pitchers I saw on the Saturday afternoon Game of the Week, with Dizzy Dean and Buddy Blattner. My heroes were the hurlers who had the biggest windups. These were the men who swept their arms all the way behind them and up over their heads as they stepped back, then pivoted, kicked their front leg high, and lunged forward to deliver the pitch bent-elbowed with a long stride and a high-kicking followthrough. I likened pitchers to car models. Warren Spahn was a DeSoto, because he swept his arms back as high as a DeSoto's soaring fins. Billy Pierce and Whitey Ford were Imperials, the next highest. Don had a nice big windup, maybe not quite an Imperial, but probably a Cadillac. Those who delivered with compressed windups and low leg-kicks were Nash Ramblers. Who would want them?

I had developed a troublesome quirk in my own delivery. The final stage of my deluxe windup caused me to jerk my head back over my right shoulder, bringing my target into focus only after my arm came forward. I threw before I looked. The wildness wasn't so noticeable when I was pitching against the garage door, for I rarely missed the whole building. But playing catch with a human being was another matter. My dad would watch my pitches sail over his head or far to one side or the other and patiently turn and stroll after them, his pipe jiggling in his teeth and his mind occupied with fuel control problems or whatever.

Herb was way less patient.

"Look at *me*!" he would scream after leaping for one of my fastballs. "Quit looking over your shoulder!"

"I *was* looking at you."

"Well, I wasn't standing on Crawfordsville Road. Go get it."

"You get it."

"He who throws, goes, man."

We'd glare at each other. I'd hawk. He'd hawk. The sun would blaze.

"C'mon, man, at least help me find it."

"He who throws, goes."

Herb was way more valuable a catcher than Dad, because he would actually pretend to be a catcher. One of the many services he provided as a best friend was to get down in a crouch, waggle a finger between his legs, and make a target of his glove. I needed him.

The other good thing about Herb was that he'd put the second finger down between his legs. That was the ancient, ancestral sign for the curveball. Ever since Whitey Ford had told me not to try to do it yet, making the ball curve had been at the top of my agenda. People were always telling you not to do things in order to keep other horrible things from happening to you. Don't pop your knuckles or your hands'll get stiff. Don't eat potato skins or you'll get cancer. Don't chew gum in public or people will think you're dumb. Smoking stunts your growth. Sitting in the whirlpool will make you sterile. I didn't know a whirlpool from a fire hydrant but I knew I'd get sterile, whatever that was, if I sat in one too long. The biggest taboo in baseball was "Don't throw the curveball before you're ready."

I was ready. I needed a second pitch. But how did you make a ball curve? Information was scarce. My *Fireside Book of Baseball* contained an article, "How I Throw the Slider" by Bob Feller, but it was unhelpful, since Feller said you had to already know how to throw a curve to learn the slider. Finally, *Baseball Digest* came to my rescue. In an article titled "Seven Stars Reveal the

Straight Dope on the Curve," a reporter asked baseball's best curveballers to share their secrets. Robin Roberts, Harvey Haddix, Bob Porterfield, Sal Maglie, Carl Erskine, Mel Harder, and Preacher Roe all generously provided practical tips. Though there were nuances in style, all seven basically said the same thing: You put your index and middle fingers directly over the center of the ball and along a seam of stitches. You threw just like you were throwing a fastball but then, right when you let go, you snapped your wrist for all it was worth and the ball spun off your index fingertip, causing its path to bend just before it reached the plate. It didn't sound that hard to do. If I could master the curve, I'd be the only person on the team—probably the only kid in all of D League—with a curve. No one would be able to hit it, and when word got around that I could throw it, they'd have to let me pitch. Here was a project worth the rest of the summer.

On a sultry Friday night toward the end of August, we Speedway Giants played our final game of the season, against our arch-foes the Speedway Eagles. We played at the Tenth Street diamond—our home field—a paradise that had been hacked from a corn field a few years before. We loved it because it was the only diamond in Speedway with dugouts. Rows of wilted corn, the leaves by then limp and brown, took up again just beyond our outfield fence, tapering off into the blue haze in long even rows. Birds had stopped singing a month before. As the players threw back and forth, the ball smacking and slapping into mitts, clusters of family members excused themselves along the wooden bleachers and sat down heavily, jarring the planks. They slapped mosquitos and told each other they'd never come here again in short sleeves. Far beyond the corn, cumulus clouds rose up into muscular columns as they did nearly every afternoon now. The air was dead still. School was just around the corner.

The Eagles had made the playoffs, and we hadn't. They took the field with a smugness that we found disgusting. We were out to wipe the smiles off their faces. That's what this game was all about.

I began the game in the dugout, as usual, cheering the others on and mentally preparing myself to take the outfield in the fourth of six innings, as always. We were tied 3–3 in the fourth, when Mr. Harley called my name. I grabbed my glove and poised myself to sprint either to left field or right, whichever he said. Instead, he put a ball in my hand. "Okay, here's your chance. You're pitching. Throw to Roger's glove. Nothing fancy—just get the ball over."

I sleepwalked to the mound, where Roger, our catcher, was waiting with an expression of pure astonishment on his round face. "What're you doing here?"

"What does it look like? What are the signs?"

"We don't *have* any signs. Just get it over and try to keep Rizotto from killing it."

Roger trotted back behind the plate and crouched down as Tom Rizotto, bat in his hand, blinked at me, as surprised as everyone else. Rizotto was a good guy, mild-mannered, good at math. He lived in the new section of town, and his sister was nice. The only thing I had against him was that he was holding a bat. He was trying to take my living away from me.

I reached behind me to get the resin bag—which wasn't there—and looked at my fielders. Surprise seemed to be the universal expression on Tenth Street. I climbed to the top of the small hill of dirt, put my toe on the rubber slab, and leaned in to look at Roger. He held out his hands, palms up, like, "*Throw* it." I held the ball. I wanted a sign. Both coaches were yelling, "*Throw the ball!*" I didn't move. With a sigh, Roger dropped his index finger. I shook him off. I wanted to start Rizotto off with a curve. It made no sense to let a good hitter sit on my heater. With no choice, Roger put down a second finger and braced himself for whatever was to come. Because there was no runner on base, I swept into my full windup, flung my head back toward the corn, and let the ball loose with a violent snap of my wrist. A second later, Rizotto was down in the dirt beside the plate, clutching his shoulder and yelping with pain. Roger walked after the ball as parents on both sides yelled, mainly at each other. Rizotto jogged to first, still rubbing his shoulder.

I hit the next batter too on the first pitch. Now they were yelling at me.

I threw three pitches to the third and final batter to face me. Just before my last pitch of the 1956 season, a curve which sailed between the backstop and the Eagles' dugout, I heard this brief conversation between two Eagles.

"Hoose is a moron."

"Yeah, he doesn't even look at the batter."

"He's fast, though. I wouldn't want to bat against him."

"Me neither."

It made my whole year.

CHAPTER SEVEN

WAITING FOR THE BELL to ring in the first day of fourth grade, I slipped behind the smokestack separating Fisher School from the junior high and scanned the herd of students for Stan Purdue. I hadn't seen him all summer and I couldn't find him now. He wasn't with the thugs he normally hung out with, and he didn't show up in my class either. Later in the day, I overheard someone say he had moved away. What a break! Better still, I learned that I had drawn the best possible teacher. Tall, cheerful, and dark-haired, Miss Hazel Smith was the most beloved teacher in the whole school. Everyone wanted her. And from that very first morning, she seemed to look at me with the eyes of someone who liked and appreciated what she saw.

School became bearable, at times even interesting. One morning, Miss Smith pinned up on the wall a map drawn by someone like Columbus. Europe looked big as an elephant, while Africa was about the size of a mouse turd. We snickered. "Well, how would *you* have done it?" Miss Smith asked, hands on hips. "The explorers were trying to map a round world on flat paper. *You* try it!" We drew Speedway, from Leonard Park to the 500-mile racetrack, and taped it to the globe. It was a total mess. This launched a whole semester on projections—especially Mercator's projection. We made our own maps and stretched them over our globe, using a grid to size and orient our map features. Mr. Northcott came in every day to help us.

On Wednesday afternoons, we had wicked spelldowns, boys against girls, contests claimed with words like "antidisestablishmentarianism" (said to be the longest word in the world). Sometimes Mr. Northcott took a few of us downstairs and taught us how to play songs by ear on the piano in the audio/visual room. After heaping public praise on my oral report of *Highpockets,* Miss Smith proclaimed herself a fan of the great John R. Tunis.

All through September, the weather stayed warm enough to play ball at recess. Miss Smith let us boys run our own baseball game at the field, while she turned rope for the girls on the playground. Having been a Speedway Giant just two weeks before didn't cut me much slack at school. The other D-Leaguers knew I had gone oh-for-the-summer at the plate, and word of my late-season mound appearance had gotten around. I was still the last player chosen, and I usually had to catch. Catcher wasn't a bad position in real games, where you wore pads and a mask and got to strategize with the pitcher, but at recess a catcher just got down in the mud behind the batter and tried to keep balls from rolling to the fence. A board that could throw would have been as good.

I kept inching forward to see the ball better through my thick lenses. I never could seem to get close enough to see the ball leave the pitcher's hand. "Hoose, you moron," they said (after a year's practice, they could make it sound like the single word *"Hooseyoumoron"*). "You're getting too close to the bat. Back up." Squinting hard, I screened them out.

One morning, I was squatting and squinting when Greg Mc-Cracken rocked back on his rear foot and swung hard at a pitch. I heard a dull crack and then I was covered in blood. I fell back screaming as several boys took off for the playground. The others stood back, eyes wide. Miss Smith took one look and ripped off the bottom of her dress, pressing the scrap of cloth hard against my head. Close behind, Miss Beck, the school nurse, ordered everyone back against the fence. Teachers carried me into the office, where I stayed with Mr. Northcott until my dad arrived. A whole lot of stitches later, I was home, out of school for a week with a concussion. Greg McCracken's at-bat turned out to be my final appearance of the 1956 season, my rookie year.

From my bed, I made up letters something like this to Don Larsen in my pounding head, none of which came out right:

Dear Don,

I thought you'd want to know: I was playing catcher in a game at recess when I got too close to the batter and he swung and split my head open.

Good luck in the Series,
Phil Hoose (Darwin's son)

Or, a little better:

> Dear Don,
>
> I've been injured in a play at the plate. I'm okay, please don't let this disrupt your preparation for the Series. My best to Mickey and Yogi and the others.
>
> Phil Hoose (Darwin's son)

No, there was no way I could write to Don under these humiliating circumstances, but Dad must have written him, because a few days later a small square box bearing a New York postmark arrived in the mail. From a soft nest of New York newspaper pages, I extracted a baseball signed by all the Yankees. It was an official American League baseball, as certified by the stamped signature of league president William Harridge. The Yankees had signed it in blue-green ink, which smeared to the touch. The ball, made in Haiti, smelled new and fresh. It bore an official-looking seal, enclosing the stamped word "Ready," meaning, I supposed, that several layers of inspectors had looked it over and passed it. On the other side of the ball from Harridge's name, in the spot where the stitching narrows, there were only two signatures: Mickey Mantle and Yogi Berra. Everyone else signed around those two. The ball came with a postcard bearing the usual image of Don following through, with a brief get-well-soon message on the other side.

I closed my eyes and tried to imagine the signature scene. They're in the Yankee locker room, probably about September 17, the day the Yanks clinched the American League pennant. Towels are being snapped. Shaving-cream fights have erupted. Mantle's

The ball Don sent me, with Mickey's and Yogi's signatures centered

on his belly in the trainer's room, his legs being taped. The brain trust is in the Old Man's office, going over the lineups for that day's game. Don, seated on the stool in front of his locker in his underwear and number 18 blue-and-white T-shirt, is leafing through his mail. Suddenly his eyes focus on a letter in my dad's handwriting with our return address in Speedway. He rips the envelope open, only to learn the devastating news of my injury. All ballplayers have boxes of balls near them; everyone knows it's one of the chores of being in the big leagues—signing balls. They grumble about it as if this was a jail sentence, but if you said to any minor leaguer, "Hey, you can go up to the majors but only if you agree to sign balls—is that too big a burden?" of course every farmhand in history would wear his hand out signing.

Anyway, Don grabs a ball from his private box, taps a beer bottle with a spike file, and brings the locker room to order. At this point, Don has won four straight starts with his patented new no-windup delivery, so he instantly commands the attention of everyone. Besides, it's pretty rare when Gooney Bird looks serious. Everyone knows there's something wrong. This isn't going to be a reading from a comic book.

"Boys," he says, clearing his throat, "it's about Phil, Darwin's boy. He's my cousin out in Indiana. Most of you met him in Chicago. Remember?" There are murmurs of recognition. "He's been injured in a ballgame. His head's been split open. Yes, it's a concussion, but they closed the wound and they think he'll be all right." A collective sigh is heard. Now Don holds up a ball. "I need everyone here to sign this before you take the field today. I wanna see your best handwriting." Mantle, overhearing Don's address from the training room, swings his aching legs over the side of the table and stumps over to Don's locker. "Gimme that ball, Gooney. I'll be the first to sign." Subdued, each with deeply furrowed brows, they line up with Yogi right behind Mick (that's why Berra's signature is squeezed in with Mantle's in the showpiece place on the ball). And now, here, a week later, it was in my hands as I lay back on the couch and rolled it over and over in my fingers, trying not to smear the most beautiful signatures in the world.

Out of school for a week and with time on my hands, I decided to take up smoking. I had plenty of models in my life. A couple of a dozen times a day, Mom slipped a Kent from a pack, clamped her lips on the Micronite filter, put a match to the opposite end, and hollowed her cheeks before filling the room with smoke. My grandpa practically sucked his Camels inside out.

Dad took up his pipe in the Navy, jamming it bowl-out into the back pocket of his dungarees, as he called jeans. At first he kept forgetfully snapping off the bowls whenever he leaned into something hard on his ship's deck, but by the time we got to Speedway he had mastered all the elaborate rituals of pipe-smoking. You could always count on Dad to reach for the pouch when someone asked him a question he didn't particularly want to answer, something like "Can I have a raise in my allowance?" He could prolong such moments forever with his pipe. He'd sprinkle water on the tobacco to freshen it. Then he'd knock out the old ashes on something hard, open his knife, and painstakingly scrape out the ring of scum remaining. By the time he'd filled up and tamped down the new bowl, smoothed it, and lit it, either he would have a dilatory answer composed, or you'd have forgotten your question.

But in the end, it was the ballplayers who made me see the advantages of cigarette smoking. I had a scrapbook full of Camel ads, strips of photos of big-leaguers wearing suits and ties and triumphantly holding freshly lit cigarettes up for the camera. I studied their smoking styles. Yogi Berra and Billy Pierce trapped the cigarette near the knuckles between their index and long fingers. Johnny Logan, Warren Spahn, and Richie Ashburn scissored it delicately at the tops of their fingers. They looked like girls. Hank Bauer and Bob Grim choked the cigarette hard between their knuckles and held it up vertically, almost as if they

One of the Camel ads that inspired my smoking adventure (from left to right, Warren Spahn, Jackie Jensen, Whitey Lockman, and Tommy Byrne)

were giving the photographer the finger. Tommy Byrne pinched the butt between his thumb and index finger and grinned into the camera. That's how I would do it.

Mantle was a Camel smoker, too, and I had a photo of Don with an unidentifiable cigarette in his hand, probably a Camel. To a man, these ballplayers reported that smoking helped them relax. They all enjoyed the mildness of a Camel. A cigarette before a game helped them perform better, and a butt in the locker room afterward helped them unwind. As Mickey Mantle put it, "For mildness and flavor, you can't beat Camels!" It all made sense to me. Learning to smoke might not only help me relax—and God knew I needed to relax—but also to fit in on the Giants, as spitting had. I had put a lot of time into learning to spit properly. I had a natural gift for eject-ing spittle through my teeth, but it had taken me months to blow a snuffled ball of snot with a soft fluff rather than a rasping *p-p-p-t*. It had paid off. Now I could hawk with anyone on the Giants.

There were smoking stories in some of my baseball biographies too. In one book about Warren Spahn, for instance, there was a great scene in which Warren's dad caught Warren smoking behind an outbuilding out in Oklahoma. Mr. Spahn's punishment was not to snap off a willow stick, or to force Warren to clean out the manure from the stalls, or to take away the keys to the truck. No, instead Old Man Spahn handed Warren a baseball, turned his back and paced off sixty feet. He squatted in the dust, faced his boy, and cupped his bare hands. "Throw it, son, as hard as you can," he commanded softly. "No, Dad, I'll break your hand," Warren protested. "Throw it!!" thundered the old man. And Warren did. And Mr. Spahn caught it! Barehanded. I couldn't quite see the point of the punishment, since Mr. Spahn could have gotten his hand practically torn off, but it was, as *Sport* magazine would have put it, a helluva story. No way Warren didn't take something off of the pitch, though.

One night during my week off from school, Mom and Dad went out for something and left me home alone. As soon as I heard the Plymouth drive off, I shouldered open the bathroom window, hoisted a fan into the space, and turned it on. I climbed onto the toilet seat so I could see my whole body in the mirror, and fished from my jeans pocket the crumpled Kent that I had smuggled from my mom's purse. I wasted at least a dozen matches before one finally caught fire. Removing my glasses, I looked into the mirror, pinched the butt, grinned like Tommy Byrne, and inserted the Micronite filter between my lips. I applied the match to the other end and sucked hard. Seconds later, I was doubled up on the stool, coughing so loud that I almost didn't hear the Plymouth swing into the driveway. Gasping and hacking, I grabbed for the fan to clear the smoke, but dropped it. It writhed around on the floor in crazy circles as I stumbled to the front door and threw the bolt shut to buy time. I flushed the toilet to drown out the sound of my coughing and locked the bathroom door. By the time Mom and Dad rattled at the front door, walked down the driveway, and came in through the back, I had blown the smoke out the window and flushed the evidence down the toilet. I was reading in bed when they found me. "Why was the front door locked, Phillip?" Mom said. I cleared my throat several times before I could answer. "I don't like being home alone," I said hoarsely, and turned back to my book.

I had no choice but to chalk up this experiment as an incomplete.

Sidelined from playing and with a head still full of stitches, I turned my full attention to the majors as the World Series drew near. The Yanks had already clinched the American League pennant, but the NL flag was still up for grabs, with three teams—the Dodgers, Reds, and Braves—racing for the wire. It was now clear that Mantle wouldn't break Babe Ruth's record of sixty homers in a single season. Mantle had stayed ahead of Ruth's pace through August, but the Babe had walloped seventeen circuit clouts in the month of September 1927, and Mantle couldn't keep the pace. With the world watching his every swing, he fell far behind.

It seemed like Don had had three separate 1956 seasons. He got off to a wonderful start, winning his first four games. Then he began to dig his own grave by walking prodigious quantities of batters. The *Sporting News* said his control had suddenly "deserted him." Discouraged, he muttered to a reporter that he was thinking of joining the Navy. There was talk of banishing him to the minors so he could rehabilitate himself, or, even worse, of "relegating" him to the bullpen, the eternal glue factory for washed-up starters. (I never heard the word "relegated" applied to any other context than the bullpen. If you got straight F's, you weren't relegated back to third grade. Your angry parents didn't relegate you to your room. No, the only possible destination for a relegatee was the bullpen, a place starters would do anything to avoid.)

Then, late in August, Don came up with a bizarre idea. According to the *Sporting News,* while pitching against the Red Sox, he grew to suspect that Red Sox third base coach Del Baker was stealing his pitches. Larsen sensed that Baker could detect what kind of pitch Don was about to throw by looking at the way he gripped the ball at the top of his windup, when it was out of his glove and in plain public sight. Baker somehow flashed a signal to the batter, who made Don pay. Realizing that he needed a foolproof way to conceal his grip, he started throwing without winding up at all. The ball was exposed for only a split second just as Don was about to bring his arm forward, leaving Baker no time to signal. Overnight, Don won four low-hit games in a row and started a minor fad. A second Yankee pitcher, Bob Turley, scrapped *his* windup too and pulled out of a slump. Suddenly essays in baseball magazines hailed Larsen's new no-windup delivery as a stylistic breakthrough. I felt like gagging when I read this garbage. I loved windups. What had happened was that my cousin, a man who once pitched like a Cadillac, had gone out and turned himself into a Rambler.

During my convalescence, I was relegated to the couch, with one exception: church. Though I held my head and moaned, when the Sabbath came around there were no ifs, ands, or buts about it. I pulled on my best clothes, held still while my mother clipped a bow tie on me, and climbed in the back of the Plymouth.

I had already had a ton of religious training. As a little kid, I had knelt with Mom each night before bed to recite a four-line prayer that often terrified me into blanket-clutching sleeplessness. The key line was, "If I should die before I wake." *"I'm not gonna die before I wake up, am I?"* I would ask her. "No, no, honey, that's just how the prayer goes," she would soothe, tucking me in. In South Bend, I had spent my summer days at Vacation Bible School. At the conclusion of each day, we Bible scholars charged blinking out into the sunlight two by two, arms linked, singing "Onward Christian Soldiers" as our waiting parents beamed. Still, my parents never really seemed all that religious. We didn't say grace at dinner, and we rarely mentioned God or Jesus around the house, but for some reason taking me to church was important to them.

Maybe they sensed that I had doubts about God. God was too much like Santa Claus, another bearded old man in the sky who knew when I was sleeping and when I was awake (he'd better have been a baseball fan) and supposedly cared if I was bad or good. I sometimes left a nickel faceup for God on the table beside my bed. "If you're real," I would pray, "take the nickel. Or match it." But unlike the carrots and cookies we left for Santa on Christmas Eve, the nickel was always there in the morning.

The Sunday after my concussion, we entered the Speedway Methodist Church, took our programs, and made our way slowly to a pew in front. The organ chirped and jittered along until everyone was seated, and swelled to fill the sanctuary with a mighty chord when the Rev. Howard W. Wright stepped to the pulpit to begin the service. Wedged between my fragrant parents, my head swaddled in a bandage that attracted the sympathy of the entire congregation, I was unusually content to bathe myself in the drowsy sunlight that poured in through stained-glass windows and listen.

That day, Reverend Wright had chosen one of my favorite stories in the Bible for his sermon. It was about the time the twelve-year-old Jesus took on the elders of the temple in a religious trivia showdown. It all started when Jesus' family went to Jerusalem with some friends for a feast at a great temple. After three days of eating and praying, the family packed up and headed back home to Nazareth, remembering everything on their checklist but Jesus. When somebody noticed the Boy was missing (I never could understand how you could lose someone with a halo), Mary and Joseph scrambled back to Jerusalem hell-bent-for-leather (as the *Sporting News* would have said) and combed the city frantically until they finally found Jesus back at the temple, which he had never left. It turned out that while everyone else was filing out of the building, Jesus had gone up and introduced himself to the elders. The elders were described as bearded old men who sat around the temple all day gathering dust and debating the fine points of religion. As Rev. Wright told it, Jesus tied them in knots. He reminded me of Billy Martin, brash but cool. Anyway, Jesus shut them all down. He could handle anything they threw his way, and before long he had them all stammering to answer questions of his own.

I deeply identified with Jesus here, as I was rapidly becoming the town expert on baseball. I was known among my parents' friends as a "walking encyclopedia." I didn't set out to become one; but I was a fast and omnivorous reader, and I took reference books practically everywhere I went. Many kids in Speedway knew racecars. I knew baseball. I could tell you the select five, the top fielders at any position, the number of lefthanders among the top ten batters of all time. When an elderly woman named Myrtle appeared on the $64,000 question, she chose baseball as her topic. I was right along with her all the way when she chickened out at $32,000. Hal March's last question was to name the six players besides Ty Cobb who had racked up more than 3,000 hits. She got it right, but who wouldn't? Cap Anson, Honus Wagner, Napoleon Lajoie, Tris Speaker, Eddie Collins, Paul Waner—it was easy.

My temple was Eddie's Barber Shop, a shack on Crawfordsville Road about a mile west of the racetrack. Dad took me the first Saturday morning of each month for my trademark butch-with-a-cowlick. Eddie and his sidekick Ralph—the elders—wore mint-green aprons and talked baseball as they evened out the heads of Speedway's boys and men.

The routine was always the same, and it continued for years. After the guy before paid, I would climb into Eddie's chair (it was an unspoken rule that I was Eddie's head, not Ralph's), let him pin the apron on me, and spin me around once. He'd say, "Bring the ears out, Phil?" and I'd reply "Same as always, Eddie." He would flick on his shaver and the battle would begin. Chubby, bald, and very loud, Eddie was a Cubs fan to his last cell. I was all Yanks. For the next fifteen minutes or so, we pitted Ernie Banks versus Mickey Mantle, Bob Rush versus Whitey Ford, the Cub double-play combo of Ernie Banks and Gene Baker versus the Yanks' Billy Martin and Gil McDougald. Eddie thought Cub second baseman Gene Baker hung the sun and moon. I would point out that Baker was leading the National League in errors at his position. Eddie would counter that that was because Baker *tried* for balls nobody else in the league could even come *near*. I would tell him it didn't matter one way or the other: The Cubs could have Tinker to Evers to Chance in the infield and their pitchers still couldn't get anybody out.

You didn't want to rile Eddie too much. When he used his hands for emphasis, his scissor blades whistled close to your head. Dad said it was a wonder I had ears at all. At the end of each session, Eddie tried to stump me on Cubs trivia, which was next to impossible. I had boned up on the Cubs after my uncle Tom had tried to convince me that Three-Finger Brown—a Cub pitcher from the dead-ball era—was actually my great-uncle. I found out it wasn't true, but it took a lot of research on Cubs history. I figured Tom probably said that to get back at the Larsen connection to the majors on Dad's side. Anyway, I could handle anything Eddie could dish out.

Men waiting for their haircuts would chuckle and glance at their watches as Eddie and I went at it. Finally he would brush the talc off my neck, unpin me, spin the chair once the other way, and fish down into his apron for a piece of gum. "He knows his stuff, that one," he'd wink at the audience, and Dad and I would walk out into the air, which felt fresh against my buzzard-bare neck.

Once in a while, usually just after school, I'd be outside pitching against the garage and my mom's voice would come through the screen, "Phil, phone call for you. It sounds like Eddie." I'd tromp in to a conversation like this.

"Hey, Eddie."

"Howsitgoin', Philboy? They doin' right by you at school? Look, we were tryin' to settle somethin' over here at the shop and thought you might help us. What was the score when Martin caught that popup to end the '52 Series?"

"Four to two."

"You sure?"

"Yeah."

"It couldn't have been three to two?"

"It could have been, but it wasn't."

"Okay then. Sure do wish it was three to two. You comin' in Saturday?"

I'd rub my head with my hand. "Naw, I was just in . . . I got a couple more weeks to go."

"All right, Phil. Take it easy."

"See ya, Eddie."

Had there been a real temple of baseball, Ray Safranka would have been the eldest of the elders. He knew more than anyone. Tall, nervous, and hatchet-faced, Ray was a high school buddy of my parents who drove down from South Bend every few weeks. He had been in the Navy, but, unlike Dad's other Navy pals, some of whom still seemed to be living aboard a ship in their heads, Ray had no interest in war stories. He was all baseball. Increasingly, it became obvious that he had come to Speedway mainly to see me. Mom would offer him dinner and Dad would hand him a beer, but he barely seemed to notice. Instead, he wanted to get down on his stomach and spread my baseball cards out over the floor and work with them. We would sort them by team, with Ray taking note of any players I'd acquired since the last time he saw me. Then we'd go down through the checklist of who I needed, and look at my doubles—surplus cards. "Trade Paul Foytack," he'd say. "You could get someone better for him."

One night Ray arrived late, with a box under his arm. As usual, he waved off food and drink, and this time he didn't even pretend to make conversation with Dad. He lowered a lidded cardboard box into our normal work space. I shooed Cinders away and scooted forward on my elbows.

"What's this?"

"Open it."

I pulled off the lid and found myself looking at several rows of baseball cards, neatly arranged, hundreds to a row.

"Wow!" I said, eyes widening. I pulled one from the middle and held it up. Joe Cronin, 1941. I had never seen a card like this. It was cardboard and about the same size as the ones I bought with my allowance every week, but the image on his card looked like a painting you'd find in an art gallery. The artist had drawn Cronin, a great old Red Sox shortstop, standing against a pink wall in his white home uniform. His form cast a lavender shadow on the wall. In the background, a chartreuse lawn gave way to pastures and hills painted in several pastel colors. A powder-blue sky was faintly visible in the distant background. Cronin's soft-featured face was filled with delicate colors. It looked as if the artist had set out to paint a ballplayer in heaven.

I pulled more cards from the box. Some were tiny black-and-white pictures of old-time players I had barely heard of—Luke

Appling, Ossie Bluege, Lon Warneke—all in black-and-white with no writing on the back. A few, called "Double Headers," had a flap that folded up to give you two players for the price of one. Babe Ruth's card was in that box, as were the cards of Honus Wagner, Ted Williams, and Joe DiMaggio. There were several cards from a 1934 series put out by Lou Gehrig.

"Where'd you get these, Ray?"

"They're my doubles. They're yours now. I'm going away for a while. You're the only person I know who will care for them right."

"Going where?"

"Just away. Keep them clean and dry and sort them any way you like, by number or team or year, though I'd do it by year. Don't let them get creased and don't handle them too much. Don't let anyone else have them. It took me a long time to collect them. They meant as much to me then as your cards mean to you now."

"Going where, Ray?"

"Don't worry about it. We'll talk when I get back. Take care of them. And yourself."

He left soon. I never saw him again. Later, my dad said he checked himself into a place where people went when life seemed to be too hard. He had been feeling stressed, and Dad didn't know why. Dad said we couldn't visit him. Once when I was home alone, I found Dad and Mom's high school yearbook and flipped through it, looking for Ray. He wasn't in Latin Club or chorus or band or Hi-Y. There was only one picture of Raymond Safranka, other than his tiny class photo. Naturally, he was in a baseball uniform. He was known to his classmates as a second baseman.

CHAPTER EIGHT

W E'RE NOT ABOUT to let the Yankees beat us," bragged
Dodger manager Walt Alston in the *Indianapolis Star* before the opening game of the 1956 World Series. "We like being
called World Champions." He had reason to crow. The Brooklyn
Dodgers had just swept the Pirates in the final weekend of the
season to beat out the Reds and Braves for the National League
pennant. And as maple leaves tilted softly to the ground in the
first days of October, the Fisher school playground became a rag-
ing battleground of mouthy, opinionated kids at full throttle. I
was at the epicenter.

"Yanks don't stand a chance."

"You're a moron."

"Snider's better than Mantle."

"You're an idiot *and* a moron."

"Your cousin sucks."

"Tell me about your cousin on the Dodgers."

"Your cousin won't even get to pitch."

"Leave me alone. You're an idiot and a moron *and* a butthole."

The debates raged. Who was better? Yogi or Roy Campanella?

At shortstop, Pee Wee Reese or Gil McDougald? Jackie Robinson versus Andy Carey at third? Junior Gilliam versus Billy Martin at second? Which was the better lineup, the Yanks with Mantle, Berra, Skowron, and Bauer, or the Dodgers with Hodges, Furillo, Campy, Robinson, and Snider? Which rotation would you take—the Dodgers with Newcombe, Maglie, Erskine, Craig, and Labine, or the Yanks with Ford, Turley, Kucks, Sturdivant, and, of course, the great Don Larsen? There was no respite to be found, even at home on Saturday morning. As I snuggled into my favorite chair to watch *Captain Midnight* on TV, I found myself repeatedly assaulted by an Ovaltine commercial reminding me that Duke Snider had smashed four homers against the Yanks in the World Series the year before.

But deep down I wasn't really worried. It didn't matter that the Dodgers had beat the Yanks in the Series in 1955. This was 1956. The Yanks had won the American League pennant by nine games, and had led since May. Mickey Mantle was better than any two Dodgers. And we had Don. No, the Dodgers weren't my problem. My problem was Mom. How was I going to get to see the games?

Mom wouldn't let me miss school. No ifs, ands, or buts about it, as she liked to say. I stormed, threatened, and pouted. I withheld affection. I refused bedtime prayers. I wouldn't eat. She wouldn't budge. I stormed out to the garage and threw a hailstorm against the door with my rubber ball, but Mom was like iron. Dad backed her up, as he always did. Miss Smith and even Mr. Northcott closed rank behind them. They all spouted a single, united party line: No staying home unless you're sick, Phil,

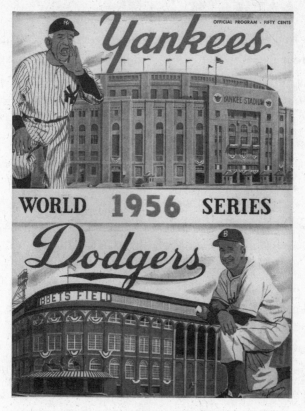

The 1956 World Series program cover

and there'll be no radio in the classroom. You're in school to learn. They acted like pods, controlled by aliens, probably aliens from Brooklyn. There was only one tiny crack in their defense: I could go home at noon, but I had to be back when the bell rang at one. And if the game was still going on after school, I could go down to the boiler room and listen with the janitors.

The Series started on a Wednesday. Since both teams were

from New York City, it would be a "Subway Series," meaning there would be no need for travel days between games. Thus the first four games would be on Wednesday, Thursday, Friday, and Saturday. I figured the Dodgers might win one, so there'd probably be a game on Sunday too. That meant three weekday games.

Mom and I sat down at the kitchen table to negotiate a plan. The goal would be to squeeze into my hour-long lunch break the maximum number of television viewing minutes possible. The games would start at noon in Indiana, since we were on Central time, an hour behind New York. I lived about a mile away from school. Mom didn't drive, so her picking me up was out. I wasn't allowed to cross Sixteenth Street on my bike alone, so pedaling to school was out too. Given all these barriers, we finally hammered out the following arrangement governing weekday games: Mom would prepare my lunch in advance—Campbell's chicken noodle soup, Oscar Mayer liver sausage on Nabisco saltines, one half sleeve of Hydrox cookies, and a glass of milk—and place these items on a TV tray in front of the set. At precisely eleven-fifty A.M., Mom would start riding my bike to the north side of Sixteenth Street. When the lunch bell rang at noon, I would fly out of Fisher School, gallop to the south side of Sixteenth, cross only after having looked both ways, leap onto the bike that Mom would be holding in place, and pedal home. The door would be unlocked. Mom would jog after.

I would watch the game until 12:43. Then without argument ("No ifs, ands, or *buts* about it") I would ride back to Sixteenth Street and ditch the bike in Mr. Rathburn's shrubs, cross Sixteenth Street (first looking both ways), and run back to school.

Mom would take my bike home and put it in the garage. It sucked, it was insane, it was crueler than any story in the Old Testament—but it was the best deal I could get.

Panting like a dog, I slid in behind the TV tray for the first game on Wednesday at Ebbets Field and realized I might just as well have stayed at school. The game was being held up until President Eisenhower could make an appearance. I was already halfway done with my soup when Ike finally came rolling through a gate in the left-field wall in a white Cadillac convertible, waving and grinning like a madman, traveling at about two miles per hour. He took forever to get out of the car and stroll to his box seat. Once there, he greeted everyone in his section by name, and finally threw out the first pitch, which was low. Then he signed the ball, shook a couple of hundred hands, and sat down. He ate up most of my lunchtime.

As it turned out, he might as well have kept pitching. Whitey Ford quickly gave up homers to Gil Hodges and Jackie Robinson, and the Yanks lost 6–3. The only good moment, right before I had to go back, was Mantle's two-run blast over the right-field screen off Sal Maglie in the top of the first.

I still wasn't worried—the loss actually was good since it guaranteed two weekend games. Besides, the Yankees still had Mantle, Yogi, and Don. The second game got rained out, and, to my delight, when I skidded in to the TV tray on Friday at noon, Don was pitching in his road gray uniform and the Yanks already had a 6–0 lead, mainly because Yogi had hit a grand slam homer in the second. I crumbled saltines into my soup as Gil Hodges led off for the Dodgers in the bottom of the second. What happened next almost made me wish I had stayed at school. Hodges singled to right, then Yankee first baseman Joe Collins booted Sandy Amoros's easy grounder. Don walked Carl Furillo to load the bases. Roy Campanella lined a pitch into left that was caught by Enos Slaughter, but it was deep enough to score Hodges.

I hated the look of Don's no-windup delivery. He sort of pushed the ball into his glove, gathered it into his stomach, lunged forward, and threw. It looked like he was tossing darts. There didn't seem to be much power behind the pitches. Why would anybody with two arms *not* wind up? They said Don scrapped the windup to keep third base coaches from stealing his pitches, but what was the difference if you couldn't get the ball over the plate anyway? The next batter, Dale Mitchell, popped up, but Don walked Junior Gilliam to reload the bases. Yogi walked out to the mound. Seconds later, emerging from the left side of our tiny screen, Casey Stengel, bent, rumpled, his arms swinging loosely at his sides, trudged out to join them. He held his hand out. Don looked pissed as he plunked the ball in. He had only given up one hit, but he'd walked four. Once again Don and I had our old friend in common—wildness. The score was still 6–1 Yanks, but not for long. Reliever Johnny Kucks immediately gave up a two-run single to Pee Wee Reese, bringing Casey back out of the dugout to take the ball from Kucks. This time he gave it to Tommy Byrne, who threw it to Duke Snider, who hit it out of the park. Now the score was tied at six.

I'd seen enough. Without even finishing lunch, I went back

outside and turned my handlebars toward school. When the three-o'clock bell rang, I ran down to the boiler room to see if the game was still going on. When I pushed the door open, our custodians stubbed out their cigarettes and sat up straight. The Yanks were way behind in the ninth, and the score ended up 13–8 Dodgers. Now we were down two games to zip. The next morning's *Indianapolis Star* reported that Larsen was "furious, despondent, and convinced that he would be banished to the bullpen" for the rest of the Series. I wasn't much happier than Don. It had taken him nearly my whole lunch break to do himself in, and it didn't look like I'd get to see him pitch again. At least they were going back to Yankee Stadium.

The Yanks tied the series by winning the two weekend games in New York. Whitey Ford and Tom Sturdivant twirled complete-game mound gems, and Mantle blasted yet another homer, a solo shot in the sixth inning of game four. This made it much easier to go back to school on Monday. Still, I found it a little troubling that each game so far had been won by the home team. According to the schedule, the Dodgers would have one more home game than the Yanks if the Series lasted seven games. The Yankees would have to win all their home games and one on the road. Don presumably watched the weekend games from deep in the Yankee bullpen. I hoped he wasn't still too down in the dumps from the second game.

When I got to the TV tray shortly after noon on Monday and lifted my spoon to start the fifth game, I was amazed to see Don back on the mound in his beautiful white home pinstripes. According to Yankee announcer Mel Allen, Don had arrived at Yankee Stadium that morning and had been startled to find a baseball in his left shoe—the ancient Yankee custom for designating the starting pitcher. Now it was already the bottom of the second in a scoreless game.

Both pitchers—Don and the Dodgers' Sal Maglie—were pitching brilliantly, and the game was whizzing by. I had read a fair amount about Maglie, since he had been one of the seven

Sal Maglie

pitchers who shared his curveball secrets with me in *Baseball Digest*. He had pitched off and on in the majors since World War II, mainly for the New York Giants. He had a reputation for toughness, some said meanness. He pitched with a heavy beard and a flat scowl on his face and was known as "Sal the Barber" because he threw so close to the batters' heads that he gave them a close shave. He was famous for his sharp-breaking curveball, but he had all his pitches working for him today. Neither Don nor Maglie gave up a hit or even a walk until the bottom of the fourth, when Mickey Mantle smacked a Maglie curveball just fair into the right-field stands. It wasn't a tape-measure shot, but a homer was a homer and that made it 1–0 Yanks after four.

After a Gillette commercial, Don walked out to the mound in the top of the fifth to face Jackie Robinson. Mel Allen pointed out that Robinson had been robbed of a hit in the second on a great play by shortstop Gil McDougald. Robinson stood in and cocked his bat, and, as Larsen set himself against the rubber, the whole stadium tensed.

"Time to go back, honey."

The sound of Mom's voice was like being shaken from a dream with cold water. This was too much. I tried to take a stand. "Mom," I pleaded. "C'mon, Mom. Just this *one* time, let me stay. It's a great game. Don's pitching. It's too close. I can't go back." I thought I saw genuine sympathy in her eyes, and for an instant I thought I had a chance. She was torn. "I just can't let you," she finally sighed. "The whole school knows where you are and why. I can't pretend you're sick. C'mon, get your jacket on."

I went back to Fisher worried to my bones and unable to think of anything but the game. Part of me hoped it would drag out long enough for me to hear the end downstairs with the janitors, but on the other hand that would mean the game had slowed down because runs were scored, which would likely have been bad for Don.

Being in that classroom on that October day was like sitting alone in a hospital waiting room while one of your parents was being operated on inside. Something huge was happening—happening to *me*—and it was out of my sight and out of my control. If Don suddenly got wild again, or got shelled, and the Yanks lost, they would be down three games to two and headed back to Brooklyn. That would be serious trouble, and Don would probably get blamed. I put my head down on my desk and tried not to think about it.

Just after two o'clock, our classroom door flew open. I looked up. Mr. Northcott made his way directly to Miss Smith's desk and asked if he could talk to the class. He seemed excited. I remember my cheeks feeling hot.

He faced us from the front of the room. "Something very special has happened," he began. "It's about the World Series. The game just ended and the Yankees won." Mr. Northcott held his hand up to interrupt the mixture of groans and cheers. "But it's far more than that. Phil's cousin has pitched the first perfect game in the history of the World Series. Does anyone know what a perfect game is?"

Of course I did, and I might have shared the information if I could have moved my lips or lifted my hand. A couple of kids blurted, "It's a no-hitter." "Partly," said Mr. Northcott, now smiling broadly. "But it's much better than that. No Dodger even got on base. Don Larsen didn't give up a hit, he didn't walk anybody, and the Yankees didn't make any errors. Larsen got every batter out in a row, twenty-seven men consecutively. The announcers are saying it's the best game ever pitched in the history of baseball. Now the Yankees are up three games to two." Beaming, he turned to me. "Congratulations, Phil."

As Miss Smith sniffled, my classmates began to applaud. Then they left their seats and clustered around my desk, pounding my back and pumping my hand. Even a few girls came over. No one stopped them at all.

In the days that followed, glory was mine. Almost all my South Bend relatives got written up in the paper, even my eighty-three-year-old great-grandma Larsen. "I watched every play of the game," she told the *South Bend Tribune,* "even the commercials." Grandma Larsen went on to reveal that none of her kids, including Don's father, had ever played baseball. Don had apparently broken the mold. "I never saw a boy who liked the game so much," she said. "In the winter when it got too cold for him to play, Don would make my son Jim [Don's dad] go down in the basement and catch for him. No wonder he's so good." That actually did explain some things. It didn't sound a whole lot different from my pitching against the garage door in the winter.

Instantly, Don Larsen's face and form and voice were everywhere you looked. He was on *CBS News* hours after I got home from school. The next morning, Dad shook me awake early to

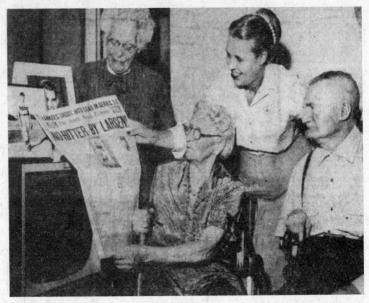

Three of Don Larsen's grandparents and his aunt look at the *South Bend Tribune* headline (seated: Mr. & Mrs. William Brown; standing Mrs. Jennie Larsen and Miss Jean Larsen)

watch Don chat with Dave Garroway on the *Today Show.* A large chunk of the morning's *Indianapolis Star* seemed to be about him.

The next day's game was almost as good. The teams went back to Ebbets Field for Game Six, with Bullet Bob Turley matched against the Dodgers' Clem Labine. For nine innings, neither team could score. Turley, like Don, pitched without a windup, and I had to admit there must be something to it if the two of them could keep the great Dodger hitters so completely off-stride. But in the bottom of the 10th inning, Turley walked Junior Gilliam and the Dodgers sacrificed him to second. Turley intentionally walked Duke Snider to set up a force. Then Jackie Robinson smacked an inside pitch just over Enos Slaughter's glove and against the left-field wall to give the Dodgers a 1–0 win. "It was the best game I ever pitched," Turley sadly told a reporter the next day. "And I lost."

The final game was a beautiful rout, with Yogi hitting two homers to lead the Yanks to a 9–0 win and the World Series victory. Elston Howard also homered, and Moose Skowron hit a grand slam. Johnny Kucks pitched a three-hit shutout. I felt jubilant and relieved to have won. Not only had the Yanks whipped the Dodgers, but my cousin was the hero of the World Series. Now I could look anyone in the whole school right in the face, as long as I didn't look too long at the toughest kids.

Day by day, it just kept getting better. First came all the newspaper photos of Don grinning behind the wheel of the two-tone Corvette he had just won as the Most Valuable Player of the 1956 Series. And then, for a month or so, you just couldn't miss him, no matter where you looked. I opened a magazine to find Don with his *own* Camel cigarette ad, not just another head shot in a strip of smoking ballplayers, but just Don, standing by himself in front of a truck filled with Camels, grinning as if he owned every last butt in the rig. One night he appeared on the *Bob Hope Show,* lobbing baseballs to Hope. The other guests were Lucy and Desi, James Cagney, and British blonde bombshell Diana Dors. Later, when *Life* magazine published a photo of Don sharing drinks and dinner at Danny's Hide-A-Way with "nightclub singer Audrey Armstrong," my classmates elbow-jabbed me as if I had been out with Miss Armstrong myself. A couple of weeks

Still smiling, Don leans on a globe after a TV appearance

after the game, newspapers published the text of an admiring letter President Eisenhower had written to Don. Finally, a month
or so later, several 8×10 photos showing Don in the locker room
after the game arrived in our mail, all signed by Don.

Things changed a bit for me in Speedway after that. Don
Larsen's perfect game gave me a small but detectable break in
the town, a little bounce in my ratings that persisted into the following spring. His heroic stature and the glory it reflected on
me, however undeserved, gave me about a season's breathing
room to learn the game, now with the help of kids who were

willing to teach me—or at least to be seen with me. In a way, this inadvertent gift was far more valuable than the postcards, the hat, the ball, the glossy photos, and the trickle of Larsenalia that continued to arrive from time to time over the next few years.

I saw Don twice more during my boyhood. The first time was in Indianapolis, after he had been sent down to a minor league team in Dallas in 1960. They came in to play the class AAA Indianapolis Indians. Dad, Mom, my new brother Tim, and I sat in half-empty stands and tried to ignore the drunks behind us heckling Larsen as "washed up" and a "has-been." Dad is slow to anger, but I felt his blood boil as these idiots became more brazen and caustic by the inning. After the game, we had our traditional brief but cordial parking-lot chat and good-bye hug before an idling bus. I remember hoping with all my heart that Don would soon be called back up to the major leagues, and he was.

In 1962, we drove to Cincinnati and watched Don pitch an inning of relief for the San Fransisco Giants against the Reds. It was an unforgettable performance. He entered the game in the ninth, assigned to protect a slim Giant lead built mainly by two Willie Mays homers. Don faced three batters, retiring each on a mighty blast to the warning track, one to left, one to center, and one to right. He couldn't have thrown more than five pitches and surely didn't break a sweat, but outs were outs and he graciously accepted the handshakes and buttslaps of his teammates as he trudged off the field. After the game, we waited for Don outside the stadium, had our traditional chat, parted with hugs, and waved as we watched the bus disappear. That was the last I would see of Don Larsen for a long, long time.

As baseball scholars surely know, I never made it to the big leagues. In fact, I topped out my baseball career as a fifteen-year-old Pony Leaguer, wearing the mammoth Spalding glove Don gave me in 1957 for my birthday. It was the only glove that could have made me remove my Wilson A2000, and I wore Don's glove until it fell apart. I did become a pitcher, and a fairly good one. My out pitch was a sweeping curveball, which started breaking, just as Whitey Ford had predicted, only when I was ready. Readiness arrived in my thirteenth year.

I've had many wonderful days since as a baseball and softball player, days that have brought me fun and excitement and many of my closest friends. But there's never been a day to match October 8, 1956.

"It's amazing," Don Larsen told a reporter a few days after pitching his masterpiece. "Not long ago I was a nobody, and now everybody wants me."

In the fall of 1956, when I was having trouble taking root in a tough new town and the game of baseball was all the world to me, I knew exactly what he meant.

CHAPTER NINE

I LANDED IN SPOKANE, Washington, picked up my rental car, and spread the Idaho map out over my lap. My finger traced a route northward through a narrowing set of highways and roads to the lake my dad had described as a "fishing paradise." "If you don't see at least one moose, bear, or elk on a day in this country, you're having a bad day indeed," said a local real estate ad on the map's border.

I hadn't seen Don Larsen in forty-three years, not since saying good-bye in Cincinnati. Over the years we had corresponded lightly, usually triggered by my asking Don to sign something for this charity or that. He had never declined, and always returned the signed object with a brief but pleasant message. He knew that I had become a writer, mainly because my article about the two of us had appeared in *Sports Illustrated*. He remained close to my dad. Now when I called to propose a visit while I was out West on business, he seemed content enough to oblige, provided we could find a date. It wasn't easy. Seventy-six years old at this writing, Don still maintains a heavy calendar of hunting and fishing trips, autograph shows, and other engagements. He was able to scratch my name into an open day just before his annual fantasy camp in Fort Lauderdale with Yogi Berra—if I could get there in time.

"So, how do I find you?"

"That's Corrine's department," he said, handing the phone to his wife of forty-eight years. She was at this moment hosting a living room full of forty women, so she quickly rolled off precise directions from the Spokane airport as I scribbled madly. Now I compared these barely legible notes against the map one final time, pushed the tripometer, and set off through bear and moose country. I hoped I'd find an ex-Yankee pitcher at the other end.

A few days before visiting the Larsens, I had traveled to Cooperstown, New York, to see how Don Larsen's career had been documented in the National Baseball Hall of Fame. A research librarian had laid out the facts on the telephone: "It takes more than a lifetime 81–91 record to be inducted. But because his perfect game *was* an immortal event, we keep Don Larsen files. Yeah, we have quite a bit of stuff. It'd probably be worth it for you to come."

I especially wondered how the perfect game's reputation had held up over almost fifty years. Back in 1956, experts had instantly crowned it the greatest pitching performance of all time. Not only had it been the first and only no-hit game ever pitched in post-season play, it was *clutch*. Larsen had saved the Yankees in a pivotal game of the World Series against a team of great hitters. Had he failed, the Yanks would have fallen behind three games to two and headed across town to Ebbets Field for probable oblivion.

But reputations fade quickly and memories are short. During my drive to Cooperstown, a radio piece reported that Ronald Reagan had been voted the Greatest American of All Time in a poll conducted by the Discovery Channel. Other Top 100 finalists included Tom Cruise, Brett Favre, Rudolph Giuliani, Hugh Hefner, and Ellen DeGeneres. Four Bushes made it, but no Adamses. Lance Armstrong was in but Louis Armstrong was out. Marilyn Monroe beat out James Monroe (and Earl Monroe, for that matter). Expert commentators suggested that a "time bias" might be at work. In this light, I wondered if anyone could still value—or even remember—what Don Larsen had done so long ago.

I also hungered to see the whole game at last. Many lesser games had been televised as classics, but after my three lunchtime innings on the day of the game, all I had ever seen of Larsen's perfect game was a clip or two, usually of Mantle's running catch off Gil Hodges's long fly ball in the fifth inning and then, at the very end, of pinch-hitter Dale Mitchell's bat freezing, umpire Babe Pinelli's right hand jerking up, and Yogi Berra running out to leap onto Larsen's massive frame. I wanted to see the excitement build throughout the whole nine innings. I assumed the Hall of Fame would have a DVD at their fingertips in a film library.

I was corrected on that score at once. Cooperstown's film archivist informed me that the actual TV broadcast films of World Series games were cut up into brief highlights and destroyed within days after the final game of the series every year between 1947—the first year the Series was televised—and 1969. Just before they were snipped, the broadcasts were preserved by kinescope—filmed and copied onto half-hour-long reels—and shipped overseas for viewing by Armed Forces personnel. However, by agreement between NBC and Major League Baseball, the kinescopes too were destroyed after a brief run through the military bases. The idea was to keep anyone from showing them for admission. A historical demand for visual recordings of entire games was unanticipated—what future American would sit there and watch a whole game? Home movie film was very expensive back then and came in reels that were typically only a few minutes long, so fans didn't record the games at home.

The bottom line is astonishing: There is almost no visual record of the first two decades of the televised World Series. In fact, the Hall of Fame possesses kinescopes of only two World Series games played between 1947 and 1969—games six and seven of the 1952 Series between the Yankees and the Dodgers. However, kinescopes of a handful of additional games have survived, rescued from destruction and smuggled back home by enterprising servicemen. Every now and then, metal canisters containing the kinescope reels crop up in odd places. One of the survivors is Don Larsen's Perfect Game—or at least most of it. According to the private collector who bought Larsen's game, five of the six canisters containing its kinescope reels turned up around 1990 in an Oregon flea market. The first reel is missing—depicting the first inning—but the rest of the game is there. The collector says he bought it for "a song." He has not yet allowed the canisters out of his basement archives.

A Cooperstown research librarian handed me a set of head-phones and ushered me into a viewing room. I slipped in a DVD of the final two 1952 World Series games, sat back, and entered another dimension. Baseball hadn't changed that much—it was still "chess at ninety miles an hour," as author Roger Kahn put it—but the world on which it was played seemed to be rotating in a lower gear. The games were played in daylight but telecast in dull black and white. Men wore dark overcoats and fedoras. Al-most everyone smoked. Tri-colored bunting was hung in scal-lops over the lower grandstand railing. As the air warmed in Yankee Stadium, customers in the field boxes draped their top-coats over this railing, causing Yankee announcer Bob Sheppard (some things never change) to intone, "Will the people in the front boxes please remove their topcoats from the railing." This prompted broadcaster Mel Allen to recall the time Sheppard had said, "Will the people in the front boxes please remove their clothes."

Batters advanced to the plate without helmets or batting gloves. Their Louisville Sluggers looked like bludgeons compared to the matchsticks used today. Batters kept both hands on the bat when they swung, sending them into pretzel-like contortions when they missed. Fielders used two hands to gather and trap flies and ground balls into their small, shabby-seeming gloves. Uniforms consisted of billowing blouses and baggy trousers, with numbers only—no names—on the back. Pitchers began their deliveries with elaborate windups and chorus-line kicks, hurling curves that swept laterally through the strike zone rather than darting downward.

Five years after shaking America by employing Jackie Robinson, the 1952 Brooklyn Dodgers' roster included three African-Americans—Robinson, Roy Campanella, and pitcher Joe Black—and one dark-skinned Latin player, Sandy Amoros. After all the furor surrounding Robinson, I wondered if the fans of 1952 would have been surprised to know that however multinational the game has become, Houston, the National league champions of 2005, would enter that year's World Series without a single African-American player on the squad.

Though I couldn't watch a video of Don Larsen's game, I was able to listen to recordings of both the radio broadcast on the Mutual Network and the audio portion of the telecast by NBC. Both were sponsored by the Gillette Safety Razor Company, which was offering a vest-pocket *Encyclopedia of Baseball* free with every purchase of a Blue Blade dispenser and Superspeed razor, all for the price of one dollar.

Compared to today's nonstop talkers, the announcers of 1956 said very little. Their voices resonated with tobacco and confidence. There were of course no replays, and therefore there was little occasion for analysis. You either saw it when it happened or you missed it. The primitive microphones picked up sounds only in their immediate vicinity. You could hear paper cups pop and hot dogs being hawked. Each game had two announcers, one who called the first half and the other the second half. They didn't banter, as they were almost certainly in different places.

The Mutual Network radio broadcast of the 1956 World Series' fifth game was called by Bob Neal and Bob Wolff. Neal, quick-witted and perceptive, led off. After Larsen struck out the first two batters he faced, Jim Gilliam and Pee Wee Reese, Neal observed that Larsen's control of his breaking pitches was much sharper than it had been in Game Two. He first referred to the game as a "pitcher's duel" between Larsen and the Dodgers' Sal Maglie in the second inning, and first cited the number of batters Larsen had retired consecutively at seven.

Almost every no-hitter includes several sparkling defensive plays, and Don Larsen's perfect game was no exception. The first came in the second inning, when Jackie Robinson blistered a liner to third that glanced off the glove of Andy Carey. Luckily it deflected toward shortstop Gil McDougald, who picked it up on a short hop and fired it to first, nipping Robinson "by an eyelash."

The game's early innings had the feeling of a great boxing match, with familiar competitors circling and jabbing, but with neither able to land a solid blow. At the end of the third inning, Neal observed that neither Larsen or Maglie had yet allowed a baserunner.

I tried to picture myself at that stage of the game on October 8, 1956: After three innings, I would have been mechanically slurping saltine-clotted chicken noodle soup and absently prying apart and popping vanilla-filled wafers, eyes straight ahead. Mom would have just jogged in the door, breathing hard, and would have sat down to watch with me in the living room. After catching her breath, she would have lit a cigarette. My stomach would have been knotted as Don faced the great Dodger hitters. I would be thinking that Mantle was due up next inning, and hoping he could bust one so I wouldn't have to go back to school with the Yanks tied or behind.

In the Dodger fourth, Duke Snider woke the crowd with a sharply hit drive down the right-field line that sailed just foul into the seats. A few pitches later, Don struck him out on a slider. In the Yankee fourth, Mantle stepped to the plate batting left-handed with two out and nobody on. The Dodgers shifted their infield defense to the right, sending shortstop Reese to the right of second base, with Robinson abandoning third to play in the shortstop's position. Mantle looked at or fouled off seven pitches before the swing that produced a sharp crack and an instant roar on the radio broadcast. Reflected Bob Neal when the crowd noise subsided: "Sal Maglie threw one bad pitch to the first twelve men he faced." Mantle's third homer of the series put the Yanks ahead 1–0. Duke Snider then produced another crowd roar by robbing Yogi Berra with a "great running catch" of a sinking liner, and the swiftly moving game, barely an hour old, entered its second half.

Here—Jackie Robinson leading off the fifth—was the point where Mom had sent me back to school. I had slammed the door behind me, swung my leg grudgingly over my bike, and shoved off toward school. Every batter from this point forward on the radio broadcast would be virgin territory for me. Listening fifty years later to Robinson chasing slow curves and hacking at rising fastballs, I found myself wondering why the Dodgers didn't try to bunt. They had three fine bunters in Reese, Gilliam, and Robinson, and surely they knew they were up against a hot pitcher in a tight game. But they kept whaling away at Larsen's precisely targeted pitches and tying themselves in knots.

After Robinson flied out to right, Mutual's Bob Neal reported that Casey Stengel leaned out of the Yankee dugout and gestured toward center field for Mickey Mantle to move a few steps to his right as right-handed slugger Gil Hodges advanced to the plate. It's a good thing he did. On a 2–2 count, Hodges clobbered a long high drive toward deep left-center. Mantle took off sprinting at the crack of the bat, racing back and to his right as fast as only he could. He plucked it backhanded out of the air in full lunging stride. As Neal put it, "Mantle reaches up and *grabs* it! That was sheer robbery!" Mantle later called it the best catch of his life.

The drama didn't stop there. The next batter, Sandy Amoros, smacked Larsen's third pitch down the right-field line toward the stands. During the regular season, baseball games were umpired by four men; but for the World Series, two more were added to the crew, stationed down the left- and right-field lines. The right-field umpire was the National League's Ed Runge. As the ball approached the stands, Runge straddled the line, watching carefully. When it landed, he signaled "foul" by waving his arms to the right of the line. Later, reporters asked him how far foul it had been. Smiling, he held his thumb and index finger about four inches apart.

Bob Wolff took over the radio mike from Neal in the bottom of the fifth, instantly inheriting the pressure of conflicting demands. On one hand, his job was to keep the audience apprised of the game's central story, becoming more prominent by the batter: Don Larsen was pitching a perfect game. On the other hand, it was a strict, time-honored baseball taboo never to "jinx" a no-hitter of any kind by referring to it while it was happening. This had been the practice since just after the Civil War, and baseball people took it as gospel. Wolff found himself dancing with a gorilla that was gaining weight with each pitch. All he could do was tease and imply, broadcasting like a geisha, revealing what he could without giving everything away.

A booth away, twenty-nine-year-old Vin Scully, voice of the Dodgers, was dancing the same dance as he broadcast the game to a huge NBC television audience. Scully had taken the mike from Yankee broadcaster Mel Allen in the fifth, and now he, like Wolff, had to inform his audience without jinxing Larsen. Cameramen also struggled to tell the visual story without provoking the touchy baseball gods. As word spread throughout the country, huge crowds began to mass outside any appliance-store window in the United States displaying a television set. NBC's cameramen chastely averted their lenses from the main Yankee Stadium scoreboard to avoid showing a white o under the HITS heading, focusing instead on sideline scoreboards that did not display hits.

Until the sixth, Wolff could still refer to the game as "one of the greatest pitching duels ever recorded in a Series game." But in the bottom of the inning, the Yanks scratched out a second run on singles by Andy Carey and Hank Bauer sandwiched around Larsen's superb two-strike sacrifice bunt. Now the spotlight was Don's alone, and there was no place for a broadcaster to hide.

Larsen made short work of Gilliam, Reese, and Snider in the seventh, throwing only nine pitches, and the Yankees failed to score. As Larsen walked slowly to the mound to face the Dodgers in the top of the eighth inning, the announcers simply had to say something. Wolff returned from his Gilette break with: "Larsen has retired twenty-one straight men. The Yankees have four hits. That's all there are in the game . . . There's a hum of expectancy here as the crowd keeps a careful eye on the scoreboard." Scully took the same coy tack, reporting that "Mr. Don Larsen, through seven innings, has retired twenty-one men in a row . . . two Dodgers have come very close to getting base hits." It was very subtle. Neither broadcaster said Larsen had retired *all* twenty-one batters he faced. Someone just tuning in could conceivably assume that perhaps the first batter in the first inning had walked or singled before Larsen bore down.

Jackie Robinson led off the Dodger eighth. A great competitor, he became the first Dodger to try to get on Larsen's nerves. As Larsen began his delivery, Robinson stepped out of the batter's box, seemed to dab at something foreign in his eye, and strolled back to chat with Gil Hodges on deck. It was like freezing a football kicker or a basketball free-throw shooter by calling a time-out. The crowd reacted with a Stadium-rattling boo. Robinson ambled back to the plate and several pitches later grounded softly to Larsen, who threw him out. "A lot of folks are holding on to the edge of their seat," Wolff commented, still playing poker. Gil Hodges lined hard to Andy Carey at third, and Amoros flied out to Mantle in center. Three outs to go. I pictured myself in Miss Smith's classroom, oblivious to the history at stake, worried that Don was locked in a tense struggle with the Dodgers. Probably at this moment I had my head on my desk and was trying not to get sick to my stomach.

Sal Maglie used the Yankee eighth to remind the world that he hadn't given up either the spotlight or the game. First up was Larsen. Fans jumped to their feet, clapping and pumping their fists as he walked out of the dugout toward the plate. Confetti streamed down from the upper deck. He struck out on four wicked pitches. Bearing down, and probably not at all happy with being upstaged, the Barber kept right on going and contemptuously struck out Hank Bauer and Joe Collins.

When Larsen took the mound in the ninth, pressure was so intense that the broadcasters practically had the bends. Leading off the inning, Wolff managed a pretzel of a sentence: "I just can't describe all that's going on as far as Larsen is concerned, but I'm sure that you who are listening are well informed." Scully said, "Well, all right . . . Let's all take a deep breath as we go to the most dramatic ninth inning in the history of baseball." Later, he said he'd been chewing on a cigarette and hoping he wouldn't choke on it.

Leading off, rightfielder Carl Furillo fouled off two pitches and looked at a high slider. Third baseman Andy Carey moved to his right to guard the line, a reminder that the game was still close and saving bases still mattered. Furillo fouled off two more pitches and flied to Bauer in right. Two outs to go. Batting second, Roy Campanella connected with Larsen's first pitch and sent a long foul clanging against the façade in the upper deck in left field. He stepped out of the batter's box, refocused, and then grounded weakly to Billy Martin at second.

With two outs in the ninth, pinch-hitter Dale Mitchell came out of the Dodger dugout and advanced slowly to the plate, swinging two bats over his head. It would have been hard to design a better man to spoil a righthander's no-hitter than Dale Mitchell. A lifetime .312 hitter after eleven years in the majors, the lefthanded Mitchell had a discerning eye and a flat, compact swing. He could slap the ball to any field. The Yanks played him straightaway, and each fielder went over what he would do if the ball was hit to him. Privately, each may have been praying he wouldn't get the chance to botch a perfect game. Mickey Mantle later recalled his struggle in the book *My Favorite Summer 1956*: " 'Please don't hit it to me,' I kept thinking. Then, 'Please hit it to me.' I worried about [Mitchell] hitting a sinking line drive or a bloop that would fall in front of me. I worried where I should play him." Mantle wrote that he kept looking toward the dugout for guidance as to where to play Mitchell, but no one would look his way. "They were leaving it up to me."

As I listened to the old broadcast, I found myself wondering where Mr. Northcott had been at that moment. I supposed he was downstairs in the boiler room listening with the janitors. So, why hadn't he come up to get me? Was he afraid he'd miss something if he left his post and ran upstairs? Was he worried I'd get too upset if I found about something so big too abruptly? Or could it have been that he got to the game late and didn't realize what was happening, since the announcers weren't saying? I'll never know.

Mitchell stood in against Larsen. He took a ball outside, and then took a slider that caught the outside corner. With the count 1–1, Mitchell swung and missed at a low slider. Now the Dodgers were down to their last strike. Defending the plate as best he could, Mitchell slapped an inside fastball foul and stepped out of the batter's box, giving the nation time to catch its breath. As Vin Scully put it, "Yankee Stadium is shivering to its concrete foundation right now."

Larsen stepped away from the mound and picked up the bag of resin near the pitching rubber. Wolff fell silent and let the solid sheet of crowd noise do the talking. Scully likewise simply seemed to open the booth window and stick the microphone out into the crowd. It was brilliant reporting. As Larsen stepped back on the mound to face Mitchell, the wall of sound that thundered through the great stadium as everyone rose to their feet wasn't just the voice of a no-hitter; it was the sound of what baseball meant to America then. "I'll guarantee you," said Wolff, "that nobody but nobody has left this park and if somebody did leave early, man, he's missing the greatest."

Yogi Berra signaled for a fastball and went into his crouch. Larsen raised his arms to his chest, tucked the ball into his gut, lunged, and threw. Mitchell took a half-swing and tried to check it. The ball whistled into Berra's glove and umpire Babe Pinelli pumped his right fist toward the sky. The huge crowd let out a cathartic roar as Scully shouted, "He *got* it! The greatest game

Yogi Berra jumping into Don's arms after the final pitch

ever pitched in baseball history by Don Larsen! A no-hitter, a perfect game in the World Series! . . . Here in New York, the most dramatic baseball game ever played. No runs, no hits, no errors . . . in fact, nothing at all." And, at the moment that Mr. Northcott was surely racing upstairs to open our door and change my life, Bob Wolff concluded his radio broadcast by saying simply, "Man, what a thrill this is."

Combing through the Hall of Fame's magazine and newspaper files, I found two themes to the post-perfect-game reportage. One addressed the sheer excellence of Larsen's performance. One reporter began his report with a single strand of adjectives: "tremendous, superb, gorgeous, wonderful, magical . . . perfect."

Joe DiMaggio wrote, in a newspaper column, ". . . this was absolutely the best pitched game I've ever seen as a player or spectator and that takes in some great pitchers and some wonderful performances." Jackie Robinson agreed that he had never faced a pitcher so commanding. Yogi Berra promptly went out and had his catcher's mitt bronzed. Columnist Shirley Povich of the *Washington Post* reported that "Larsen's tremendous assortment of pitches . . . seemed to have five forward speeds, including a slow one that ought to have been equipped with backup lights."

The other theme was the perfect game's unlikeliness, especially given the source. One reporter, groping for something novel to ask Larsen in the locker room, wondered, "Is this the best game you ever pitched?" The question's sheer absurdity made several news stories: Larsen had entered the game with a lifetime record of 30 wins against 40 losses and was best known for his wildness on and off the field. The headlines told it all: IMPERFECT MAN PITCHES PERFECT GAME; HOOSIER PLAYBOY STUNS DODGERS; BAD BOY MAKES GOOD. The composite image of Don Larsen was that of an overgrown child, a prisoner of vast appetites with a special sweet tooth for liquor, women, and comic books. The *Saturday Evening Post* described him as "a real-life Little Abner." He called himself "Night Rider." He supposedly told his teammate Mickey McDermott that the "Ghouls" from his comics had signaled him that it was okay to pitch without a windup.

But there was said to be a thoughtful side too. Stengel didn't much care for his hours, but found him hard-working. After the game, Larsen spent $1,000—a substantial sum in 1956—buying commemorative plaques for his teammates as a way of thanking them. He confessed that between those final pitches, he was thinking about his parents, who must have been watching him somewhere. He was said to be intensely loyal to anyone who had ever helped him, and more at ease with ordinary people than with the celebrities he was suddenly meeting. He was said to take in stray pets.

And how had the perfect game's reputation held up? At this writing, there have been eleven more perfect games pitched (all during the regular season) since Larsen's accomplishment, bringing the historical total to seventeen. A few of them were more commanding than Larsen's, especially Sandy Koufax's fourteen-strikeout performance against the Cubs in 1965. But most were hurled in meaningless games (all but three of the regular-season perfect games have been pitched in April, May, June, and July). Many were pitched against weak lineups, such as the lowly Cubs Koufax faced, who finished 1965 with a 72–90 record.

There have been many masterful individual pitching performances, including scores of no-hitters and high-strikeout games. Roger Clemens and Kerry Wood each struck out twenty batters in a nine-inning game. Twenty-two-year-old Johnny Vander Meer pitched two no-hitters in a *row* in 1938. Pittsburgh's Harvey Haddix pitched twelve perfect innings against the powerful Milwaukee Braves in 1959, retiring thirty-six batters consecutively before losing the game in the thirteenth inning. There have also been brilliant performances in high-stakes games, such as aging righthander Jack Morris's ten innings of shutout ball to win the 1991 World Series for the Minnesota Twins against the Atlanta Braves, and—my personal favorite—the one-hit, seventeen-strikeout shutout that Boston's Pedro Martinez pitched against the Yankees in September 1999. Pedro was so commanding that the Yanks managed to hit only one ball fair after the fourth inning.

But when one combines a pitcher's command of the batters he faced in a game, the difficulty presented by the opposing lineup, and the importance of the contest, Larsen's feat stands alone as the greatest game ever pitched. Since 1956, few have even come close to pitching a no-hitter in post-season play, much less a perfect game, even though the playoff system has been greatly expanded. Four of the batters Larsen faced on October 8, 1956 are now in baseball's Hall of Fame—Jackie Robinson, Duke Snider, Pee Wee Reese, and Roy Campanella—and a fifth, Gil Hodges, should be. And the game was as important as a game could be.

Still, though Don Larsen pitched all or part of fifteen seasons in the major leagues and won a total of four World Series games against but two losses, he is not Roger Clemens or Sandy Koufax. Thus, Don Larsen's perfect game has settled historically into the category of a "miracle," a baseball monadnock isolated in history but steadfastly resisting erosion. In Cooperstown, Larsen's feat is regarded as the baseball equivalent of Bob Beamon's long jump in the 1968 Olympics—a phenomenal achievement that came without precedent or context, something that defies statistical analysis. It just happened. The accomplishment is celebrated, but its author is not enshrined. It is something wonderful that cannot be explained, a magical event that will keep heads shaking forever.

As I drove home from Cooperstown, I wondered who I was

going to meet in Idaho: Night Rider? Little Abner? The Consummate Professional? The Family Member who Broke the Mold? And who would I be?—the nine-year-old or the fifty-nine-year-old? Was there a difference?

I pulled up to a tri-level ranch house backed up against an inlet to a lake, checked the house number against my directions, and put the map away. As I bumped my suitcase along the stone walkway up to the Larsens' front door, I noticed that each step bore the stenciled image of a frog.

Corrine answered the bell, and welcomed me with a smile and a hug. She is youthful, trim, and pretty. "Don's right back here," she said, leading me across plush white carpeting toward the kitchen. She stopped at the kitchen door and smiled, as if presenting me to someone. I looked around, but didn't see a soul. And then, as my eyes adjusted to the dim light, I made out a figure, backlit by brilliant late-morning sunlight, seated at a kitchen table. The man, huge, rounded, in a salmon-colored shirt, kept his back to me. I walked around and looked at him. The face was more deeply lined but familiar, with blue eyes, long sideburns, and a somewhat-thinning-but-still-impressive head of silver hair, much like my dad's. The Larsens keep their hair. It's a shame the Browns didn't, I thought—I might still have some. He put out an enormous hand and looked up. "Hi, cousin," he said.

Laid out before him on the kitchen table were a half-dozen cheroots, a quantity of dog biscuits, a Sharpie, and a pile of envelopes, photos, and other objects to autograph and mail. His chair was positioned beside a screen door, kept open a crack even though the air was cool because Corrine dislikes the odor of the cheroots. On the other side of the door, a chocolate Lab named Colt lay stretched out on a deck overlooking the lake. Now and then, Don would pull back the screen and hand out a milkbone or two. Colt didn't budge far from the door.

We made small talk for a while, Don in a gruff, flat voice. Then Corrine stood and said, "Well, I'll let you cousins catch up," and off she went. Don's eyes followed her out the door, and I wasn't too comfortable myself. What was I doing here? He poured us each a drink and we launched the afternoon.

I asked him if he could actually still remember anything of what it felt like to be on the mound that day. "Sure, I can still feel it," he said. "I think about it at least once or twice a day, and I can still see it. It was a good day for me. Everybody's entitled to a good day. You work hard enough, sometimes it'll come true. My second-best day? Meeting Corrine." The two good days came very close together, he explained. She had been a flight attendant on a plane the Yankees took to Kansas City in 1957.

We chatted about the fact that nobody would talk to him during the perfect game, for fear of jinxing him. "Yeah, I saw Mickey Mantle in the dugout entrance grabbing a smoke late in the game," he said. "I said, 'D'ya think I'll do it?' and he walked away from me like I had the plague."

But well-worn stories don't take much time to tell. A few minutes into our talk, it seemed like Corrine had already been gone a long time. From time to time, Don got up and looked out the window. "Where IS she?" he'd ask. The Larsens' son Scott—pleasant, polite, even taller than Don—and Scott's wife Nancy came to visit, but they left too. It looked like a very long afternoon.

What I really wanted to know was how strongly connected he felt to my family—and therefore to me. The notion that this famous man was my cousin had been part of my emotional landscape now for fifty years. I pulled from my suitcase an 8x10 print of a family photo my dad had given me and laid it flat on the table between us. Taken around 1915, it's a formal portrait of a Norwegian immigrant family arranged in two rows against a flowered wallpaper print. Dressed in their finest, the Larsen parents— my great-grandparents, both born in Oslo, Norway, in the 1870s—are seated with the youngest children in front. The older children stand behind. No one smiles. In the back row center

Don's grandparents and their children. Don's father is in the back row, center

stands Don's father, Jim, a head taller than everyone else, poking out like Lew Alcindor in the Power Memorial team pictures.

Don inched his chair forward and stared at the photo. His finger came to rest first on an angelic-seeming blond boy of about ten. Positioned front and center between his parents, this chubby-cheeked boy alone wears a bow tie rather than a necktie. "That's Kay, isn't it?" Don said, tapping his image softly. "Now there's one guy I wish had seen the perfect game. He ended up looking exactly like Clark Gable—a big guy with a great head of wavy brown hair." Kahlo Larsen was a family treasure, a man whose Hollywood good looks and generous spirit brought everyone together. A South Bend police officer during the years of Prohibition, Kay steadily smuggled booze out of Canada along Lake Michigan in the back of a hearse. When he had moved enough of it, he turned in his badge and bought his own neighborhood pub, naming it "Kay's." "I was only in Kay's two or three times when I was old enough to drink," Don says, "but it was a real nice little place. And Kay was a great guy to be around."

I knew him too, since he had practically raised my dad. Kay gave Dad the keys to his convertible for his first dates with Mom. When they married, Kay loaned them the money for their mortgage. Kay's tavern united the two sides of my family. Dad sometimes took calls from my Grandma Brown to go down and fish Grandpa Brown out of Kay's and walk him back home. In his final months, just after my sixth birthday, Kay purchased a home movie camera, from which no one was safe. He promised me we'd make a movie together someday about a magic crime-fighting kid who was launched from a rocket concealed in the basement of the

Uncle Kay behind the bar in his tavern

tavern whenever Kay answered a secret phone. The last time I saw him, I asked, "So, where are we gonna show it?" Kay stood up and dumped me from his lap. "Let's go," he said. He drove us into town and stopped his convertible in front of the Colfax, South Bend's finest theater. "That's it," he said, grinning. "There's where our world premiere will be." But Uncle Kay died before we could get financing.

Don's finger moved up a row and to the right of his father, settling on Uncle Art, Gateway to the West. After he established himself in California in the '30s, Art Larsen developed extensive connections within the aircraft industry. He encouraged us all to follow. Don and I made the trip from Indiana to California to see Uncle Art a decade apart. I went in 1953 in a rented red Studebaker with Mom and Dad so Dad could interview for engineering jobs. Don went with his mom in 1944, a year after Art had found Jim a job making gunsights during World War II, and had also found a job for Don's sister Joyce. In one sense, it was a bittersweet parting for Don. "We had to put everything we had in one little car," Don recalled. "I had at least a thousand comic books, but there was no room to take them. It was a beautiful collection: Action Comics, Big/Little Books, you name it. I had baseball cards too, mainly Cubs and White Sox, with a lot of doubles. One day I had to tell my friends, 'Come over and take what you want . . . the rest are going in the dump.' God knows where they are now."

We returned to the photo. Aunt Jeanne's image reminded Don of all the times she came to see the Yankees play in Chicago. "Jeanne and Maxine, they used to come and we'd meet for a meal at the Del Prado Hotel, right there on the lake." I reminded Don of the rainout day when we came and he introduced me to all the Yanks but one. Cutting to the chase, I asked, "Why do you suppose you wouldn't let me go ask Mantle to sign my book?" "Probably because I wanted you to get the autograph," he replied, looking up. "Sometimes Mick could get a little moody and a kid could get disappointed."

After dinner, Corrine led me down a spiral staircase to "The Memorabilia Room." "He won't come down here much," said Corrine over her shoulder. "So this is one of my jobs." The room was a little chilly, but the memorabilia was abundant and superbly organized. At the center was Larsen's tent-like pinstriped jersey, number 18. A rack held several bats, a reminder that Don, always a skilled and powerful hitter, once owned the major league record for most consecutive hits by a pitcher—seven. A small library contained books written about the perfect game. There were walls full of baseball cards, scorebooks, and framed photographs, beginning with the letter from President Eisenhower ("It is a noteworthy event when anyone achieves perfection in anything . . ."). There were photos of Don with Mantle, DiMaggio, Yogi, Sal Maglie, and Walter O'Malley. It was a tasteful reminder that the guy at the table upstairs had done something quite remarkable.

The following morning, I was up early to drive back to Spokane. Corrine and I were having a talk over coffee when Don lumbered in and sat down at his chair at the kitchen table, clicking on the TV. I asked him if I could record some of the stories he had told me the day before. He quickly agreed, snapped off the set, and once again we bent over the Larsen family photo. The room shrank and softened again, and we returned to Indiana.

When we were done, Don asked me to go see if my dad's name was in his telephone Rolodex. As I flipped through it, skipping by Ralph Branca and Yogi Berra in the B section, I found my dad's name just behind the card for Tom Haller, the superb Giant catcher of the '60s. I handed Don the card and he dialed the number. "Darwin? This is Don Larsen . . ." and off they went. He concluded, to my surprise, by telling Dad he loved him. He was about to hang up when Corrine said, "Hey, Don, aren't you going to tell him who's here?"

"Oh, yeah. Phil's here. Wanna talk to him?"

Don and me in 2005

The Don Larsen I found, fifty years after I sent him my first desperate postcard for help, was many of the things people said he was: an outdoorsman, plain-spoken with a sense of fun, certainly a man of large and various appetites. He still liked to drink, still hunted frogs, still had a few comics in the basement, and was still warm to me. Ignoring the clock and perhaps a doctor or two, he had managed to outlive all but one of the Dodgers who faced him that golden day. And somehow, it seemed to me that he had met the challenge of standing up to the Perfect Game, not denying it, but not being owned by it either.

No, he didn't remember much about me as a kid, except that I was Darwin's boy, but that was good enough. He was tickled to know that his encouragement had helped me. He liked and seemed to admire my dad. It made sense to him that I had needed a little supplemental help in learning the game. "Your dad wasn't really an athlete," was how Don diplomatically put it.

We posed for a snapshot before I picked up my suitcase to go. As Corrine depressed the camera button, Don gave me a squeeze and a broad smile. I guess I had expected to find an old ball-player, a sort of half-ghost that people had always said I was con-nected to, though I had somehow never completely believed it. But there was more there, and it was solid and it felt good. I found blood. Less removed now, I found a cousin.

SINCE 1956, I have never stopped playing ball. At this writing, I'm entering my fiftieth year on the diamond. I was a hippie, a student, a graduate student, a professional. I convulsed along with the rest of society, sold out, shifted priorities and cities and teams, but I never stopped playing ball. I've played through two marriages, five wars, Watergate, several mortgages, seven books, and a great job. I played through busted shoulders and collarbones, torn meniscuses, and insults to body parts I had never heard of.

I've never stopped rooting, either. My lunchtime arrangement with Mom lasted two more years, when Don Larsen pitched against the Milwaukee Braves in the 1957 and 1958 World Series, starting game seven in both years. Though Don got traded to Kansas City in 1959 (in the deal that brought Roger Maris to New York), I remained a devout Yankee fan. In junior high and at Speedway High, my teachers replaced my mother as obstacles to watching the games, but they were no match for Mom—or me. The Yanks always seemed to be in the Series, and nothing was going to keep me from them. Game after game, my friend Dick Thomson and I would forge hall passes and present them to gullible study-hall teachers who signed us out of class. Then the trick was to escape the building. We couldn't go out the front without passing by the school office, so we went for Speedway High's distant but lightly used rear door. Flattening ourselves against the wall, ducking under classroom doors with windows, Dick and I would edge our way to the back entrance. Then we would take off sprinting across the parking lot, through the football field, and on to Vonnegut's Hardware in the Speedway Shopping Center. There, our friend Rex Crandall, an SHS alum who worked for Vonnegut's, would snap on one of the store's TV sets and watch the action with us between customers.

My baseball career ended when I saw my first adult curveball. It was thrown by a small-framed boy named Ron Kron in an all-star game in Indianapolis. After I fouled off two fastballs, Kron threw a pitch toward my head that seemed to freeze in the air. After I staggered backward, it dived neatly over the inside corner of the plate for a strike.

An instant believer, I converted to softball, first fast-pitch and then slow. In the '60s, I tied my thinning hair back with a headband and played third base for my dormitory team. I moved to New York City in the '70s and played center field for an office team in the Central Park League. Four diamonds were squeezed onto a flat meadow, arranged in a configuration that from a helicopter would have looked like an inverted cloverleaf. We twelve outfielders were backed into each other cheek to hip and back to back. Between pitches, we chatted over our shoulders and warned each other when long flies were belted from someone else's diamond. I remember one of those outfielders telling me over his shoulder that Richard Nixon had resigned.

In the late '70s, I moved to Washington, D.C., and organized the Nature Conservancy's softball team. We played at the base of the Washington Monument in a mixed-gender league. The league officials were congressional staffers who took pleasure in promulgating dozens of rules governing all aspects of play. Most involved women. At least three women had to be on the field at all times. Women couldn't bat consecutively. If a team walked a man before a woman came to bat, the man got to advance to second base. The pitcher and catcher always had to be women.

Shelley, a data manager whom we called Peaches, kindly volunteered to catch for us. Like many catchers, she had no appetite for collisions at the plate. When throws whistled in from the outfield to nail a runner, Peaches demurely stepped aside and let the ball bounce into Constitution Avenue. This enraged our second baseman, Steve. Midway through the season, he hustled in on one such play, stepped in front of Peaches, and took the throw. "You *pig*," she screamed. "That was *my* play!" "Make it, then!" Steve replied. Blood boiled. As coach, I spent much of my season mediating those two points of view.

When I moved to Maine in the mid-1980s, I joined a Sunday softball pick-up group that played near a lighthouse on the coast. Two decades later, we're still going strong. Sometimes fog makes it difficult for outfielders to see the plate, but voices carry well through cool, damp air. We play at least one game a month even in the winter, using an orange ball that shows up well against snow. Our infielders know there is no bad hop like a sharply hit ball that skips off a patch of ice. Each Sunday, we halt the game and turn around to watch the top deck and smokestack of the *Scotia Prince* drift past us from right to left, returning from Nova Scotia to its berth in Portland.

Ours is a playful and conflict-averse group of men, women, and teens. Scorning authority figures, we choose sides by drawing marbles from a bag, clears vs. blues. We bat by position, so that no one can dictate who will go last. When someone gets hurt, we pinch-run for each other, though pinch-running is governed by the (often abused) Doctrine of Roughly Equivalent Speed, meaning you can't run a greyhound for a beagle. When October comes around, we scrape aside some leaves and plant a radio on a dugout step so we can listen to the Red Sox as long as they remain alive. We're close: When one of us died not long ago, we planted a tree in his honor to the right of first base.

For me, it's the same drill every Sunday. I push back from the breakfast table, pop six hundred milligrams of ibuprofen, and wash it down with a power drink. I smear neat's-foot oil on my glove and SPF 30 on myself. I fill the water bottle, slip the donut over my bat, jam my sunglasses into the slits on the sides of my ballcap, load all this stuff onto my bike, and push off about twelve-thirty. Looking like a one-man band, I whiz over the bridge separating Portland and Cape Elizabeth, hoping the bridge won't raise and cause me to miss batting practice. At one-ten, I pedal behind the backstop, prop my bike up, and greet the other early arrivals. By then, Wendell is dragging the infield.

I stretch and throw until enough people have filtered in to take batting practice, then step in and take my twenty swings. I have lost some power, but because I have learned to line the ball to all fields I might be a better hitter now than I was twenty years ago.

I pick up my glove and run out to the field. If Mickey Mantle were still alive, he and I would have something else in common besides Lifebuoy: suspect knees. After two arthroscopic operations, I have had to give up basketball, wallyball, competitive running, and steep hikes—in order to hold out for softball. I am taking my last athletic stand in the infield.

My body is trying to retire one part at a time. Just last year, I had to give up playing third base because my shoulder would no longer let me rifle the ball overhand without sharp pain. That right shoulder had given me fifty good years, starting with the throws I made against the garage door in Speedway, but it got down to maybe two hard throws a game. I rationed them like cigarettes in a prison.

Stripped of my favorite position, I considered my options for a new home on the diamond. Outfield was out—too many sudden sprints and long throws. I could fade away to first base like an old soldier, settling for a life of lunging for errant throws and trying to remember to bring out the infield ball when the sides changed. Or I could catch; but in Sunday softball, catching can feel like shuffleboard. Second was a possibility, but every old-timer wants to play second because of the short throw to first. Why should I join the crowd?

There was one other insane alternative: Approaching sixty, I could become a shortstop. On the face of it, shortstop is not a practical semiretirement option. The ultimate multitasker, a shortstop directs the flow of energy around the infield, making more plays than anyone else while always trying to think two or three steps ahead. A good shortstop combines an air traffic controller's omniscience with a boxer's reflexes. Daunting as all that was, the position still offered two special advantages for me: you don't have to run a lot, and most of the throws are made sidearm. I can throw sidearm without pain.

So I asked Alex Gerberick, the best of our shortstops, to take me on as an apprentice. He hit me grounders on evenings after work, teaching me how to snap throws sidearm while running from various crouched positions.

I practiced just as diligently as I had against the garage back in Speedway. I packed my glove on business trips and badgered colleagues by E-mail to pack theirs as well. Scorning indoor fitness centers, I spent my breaks practicing sidearm throws in Marriott courtyards and on Hyatt lawns with middle managers, administrative assistants, and project directors.

By far the most memorable moment in my shortstop education came during a day-long strategic planning session at a Connecticut conference center. Finding myself unable to sit still by midafternoon, I stood, brushed the powdered sugar off my tie, and walked outside. Free at last, I hung my blazer on a tree limb and stretched. I picked up a stone at my feet and tried to remember what Alex had told me. Step *toward* your target. The step will guide your throw. I bent low at the waist, stepped forward, and flicked the rock sidearm at the tree twenty feet in front of me.

Way wide to the left. I picked up another. Off to the right, even farther. This was serious.

I picked up another rock and once again took the measure of the tree. I drew my arm back, bent low, and fired again. Somehow, the rock got caught in the crook of my finger and remained there until my arm had whipped all the way across my body and back over my left shoulder. It took me a split second to realize that I had thrown the rock *behind* me. I turned around and spotted it, still in the air, its flight weakening over a line of parked cars. A second later it fell through the tempered windshield of a new Lexus sedan. One tick later, it lay entombed on a leather seat beneath thousands of identically sized, green-tinted glass particles. The entire windshield had imploded.

This had to be a cosmic prank. After so many years of having thrown balls through windows, behind shrubs, off gutters, under parked cars, deep into thickets of poison ivy, how could my errant arm still be betraying me at the age of fifty-nine? Don Larsen's wildness may have diminished his career, but it hadn't affected his insurance rates. And unlike Don, I haven't yet had my one perfect day.

For a while, it looked like the family baseball line had ended with me. My brother Tim was born when I was eleven. Even though I insisted that his middle name be James, the same as Don's, when Tim got old enough to choose how to spend his time, he picked up a guitar instead of a glove. So far, he has no children. My elder daughter Hannah played a few softball games while in school, and flashed a little promise as a lefthanded hitter, but never showed serious interest in the game after that.

Through most of her girlhood, Ruby, my younger daughter, seemed to regard our outings to Hadlock Field, home of the Class AA Portland Sea Dogs, as occasions to run around looking for friends and eat ballpark food. Ruby loved the cuisine, loved Slugger the Sea Dog, fed the Trash Monster, and once got to sing "YMCA" with Slugger on the dugout roof. But she rarely watched the games.

I tried to keep the flame alive by inviting three young friends, Josh Waxman and Will and Ian Connelly, and their dads, to help me sort Ray Safranka's old baseball cards at a local bank—we called it "going to the vault." All three boys play ball, and each of them has a keen interest in baseball history. I have carried Ray's cards with me everywhere I've ever lived. I keep them in a safe deposit box along with my own cards and the 1956 Yankee ball that Don sent me. At first, the bank officials balked at my proposal that three men and three teenaged boys be allowed to crowd into one of their tiny booths to examine the contents of a safe deposit box. Then, when I explained what was in the box and what I wanted, the branch manager softened. She pinned a sheet up in front of the glass picture window to her own office so no unauthorized person could see the contents, and, after delivering the box to me, vacated the room, locking the door behind her.

Alone, we opened the metal rectangle and looked inside. There were rows and rows of faithfully sorted cards, most from the 1940s and '50s, but some from before. We carefully extracted the cardboard rectangles from the box and laid the cards out in rows on her desk. Immortal faces looked back at us from pastel backgrounds: Mays. Mantle. Aaron. Robinson. Clemente. DiMaggio. Musial—my grandpa's hero. Joe Cronin's beautiful old pastel card from 1941. Greenberg. Williams. Spahn. Koufax. And of course, Larsen. Seated around the banker's desk, the six of us ranked the players, and the boys helped me tuck the chosen cards into cellophane envelopes I had purchased to better protect them. Sifting through the cards, pulling them, aggregating them, scrutinizing the statistics on the back, feeling once again the cardboard edges against my fingers, brought back the hundreds of hours I had spent with these objects when I was young.

About half the cards in the vault were those I had collected myself. I remembered the yellow packages they came in, the furious

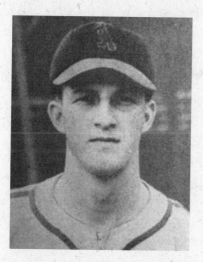

One of Ray Safranka's baseball cards pictures the young Stan Musial, one of my grandpa's favorite players

anticipation with which I tore the wrappers open, and the faintly unpleasant odor of the brittle pink slabs of gum inside (Don Larsen had actually *liked* the gum, but I found it inedible). There were six cards to a package. Finding a Mantle or a Mays, or a card that I didn't already have, produced incomparable ecstasy; six doubles could spoil my week.

Flipping the cards over at the vault, the boys and I studied rows of evenly typeset statistics. Many of the players back then played for only one or two teams in their entire careers. The cards had even columns of unbroken "St. Louis" or "Chicago—NL" or "Cleveland" under the heading "team." Though players were chattel and many—including Don—had to work in non-baseball jobs in the off-season, at least in those days a young fan could grow up with and learn to love the players on a team.

Above all, as I spent time examining baseball cards with these boys, Ray Safranka came rushing back, the feel of him, quiet and intense. Back then, I was on my belly in a tiny living room, sometimes in my pajamas, as he told me about players from a time when all the games were played in daylight. A few of his cards are nearly a century old now. All of them, his and mine, came from Indiana, and each one was thoroughly considered and deeply loved. It felt good to share them with a new generation of fans, even in a banker's office in Maine.

As satisfying as the bank experience was, I still longed for a genetic link to the game. I had just about abandoned all hope until one summer evening between Ruby's seventh- and eighth-grade years, when we were seated together in the lower boxes at Hadlock Field. She was working on a Sea Dog biscuit and I was watching the action. The game was close. There was a runner on first with one out in the late innings.

"They oughta send him," I muttered.

"Send who?" Ruby said.

"The runner," I replied, still, I thought, talking to myself.

"Who would send him where?" Ruby asked. "What do you mean?"

I looked at her. She had a scorecard in her hand, and she had made marks on it.

"Why do you want to know?"

"I don't know," she replied. "It's interesting."

Had God picked up the nickel? I assumed her interest would quickly pass, but events interceded. First, the Boston Red Sox, New England's team, took a serious run at the American League East championship that summer. They had charismatic stars such as Manny Ramirez, Pedro Martinez, and Johnny Damon. Ruby got into them. Astonishingly, I found fatherhood pulling me away from the Yanks and toward Ruby's team. She put a Red Sox scene on her screensaver and pinned a poster of Manny Ramirez up on her bedroom wall.

A second event seemed to seal her allegiance. In the early autumn of 2003, our Sunday softball group rented a bus and hired a driver to carry thirty or so of us down I-95 for an evening game at Fenway Park. Ruby decided to go, and took her friend Courtney along. We left Portland in mid-afternoon, raffling off prizes for a charity from the front of the bus during the trip. The bounty included some nice boxed CD sets and choice concert tickets, but we all coveted one prize above all others: Two vastly upgraded seats for the game. Two lucky people holding red ticket stubs with magic numbers would get to sit in golden seats just behind the Red Sox dugout, far from the rest of us in the distant, beer-soaked centerfield bleachers.

Ruby and Courtney won, and these turned out to be ducats (as the *Sporting News* would have put it) to a magical game. Baltimore jumped ahead quickly and took a 5–2 lead into the bottom of the ninth. By this time, hundreds of soul-dead fans were already slouching toward home, leaving Ruby and Courtney a clear pathway of vacated seats to the front row. So it was that at the moment Red Sox second baseman Todd Walker came to the plate with two outs and two runners aboard, the very best seat in Fenway Park, flush against the Red Sox dugout, was occupied by Ruby S. Hoose. Down to his last strike, Walker leaned into a low fastball and smacked a home run into the bullpen to tie the game. It was a shocking blast, injecting sudden hope into Red Sox Nation. From my centerfield aerie, I knew that, somewhere way down there, Ruby was but a few feet from a riotous celebration, and that she must be incredibly excited.

But it didn't stop there. David Ortiz led off the home tenth with a clout over the Green Monster, sending the now playoff-bound Red Sox players pouring out of the dugout, screaming and singing and jumping up and down. As Ortiz rounded third, Ruby, from a distance of perhaps fifty feet, was witnessing the rapid transformation of a baseball team into a mosh pit. The mammoth Ortiz leaped onto the plate, and was first engulfed and then lifted off his feet and passed overhead like a slice of pizza by his jubilant, hopping teammates.

By the time we met up with Ruby, she and Courtney were talking so fast that they could barely be understood. Totally jazzed, we all walked back to a nearby Burger King parking lot to meet the bus and head home. But the bus was elsewhere, stranded as it turned out by a dead battery, and we had lost communication with the driver. We waited for hours. By midnight, the Burger King had closed and we were all thirsty. I remained in the parking lot to look for the bus while Ruby and Courtney made their way with a few adults to Thornton's Fenway Grille, a nearby corner pub.

A half hour later with no bus in sight, I decided to go over and join them. I opened the door, and, when my eyes adjusted to the light, I found Ruby at the bar chatting with Todd Walker. Thornton's was Walker's neighborhood pub. Far too excited to

Ruby Hoose (left), Todd Walker, and Ruby's friend Courtney Ward

sleep, he had walked over to the Fenway Grille with his wife to celebrate the highlight of his baseball career. Sox first baseman Kevin Millar was with them. So was Ruby.

We didn't get to back Portland until four A.M., and I drove Ruby to school five hours later. She wasn't happy, but in a way it seemed fitting: I had had to go back to school on the biggest day of my young baseball life too. As Don Larsen had said, everyone deserves a good day. But as my mom might have added, if your good day comes on a school day, you still have to go. No ifs, ands, or buts about it.

ACKNOWLEDGMENTS

W HERE TO BEGIN? With ballplayers and fans, naturally. I thank those who have shared the game with me throughout the years, especially Dave Hall, Andy Schwarz, Eileen O'Brien, Buck Briggs, Steve Hartstack, Ben Gregg, Will Anderson, Joanne Lannin, Alan Reinhardt, Chuck Susswein, Dick Thomson, Mark Maxwell, Toby Hollander, Jon and Donna Halvorsen, Don and Stephanie Federman, and Tom Atwell. My life would be gray indeed without my current crop of Sunday Softball teammates, including Fast Tim Averill, Joseph Bacica, Wendell Clough, Pete Darling, Joe DeGeorge, Regina Erskine, Alex Gerberick, Tony Gerry, Brian Goss, Paul Joy, Jerry La Pointe, Gail M. Libby, Marianne Matte, Pete Metsch, Crystal Risbara, Mike Roland, Ray Routhier, Allen Stein, Bob Stein, Wayne Todd, Mike Turcotte, and Frank Van Sanford. I look to the future of baseball with confidence when I think of Will Connelly, Ian Connelly, Peter Stein, and Josh Waxman.

I am grateful to my Speedway High School Sparkplug classmates, especially Linda O. Maley and Chris Biltimier, for providing insights about Speedway in 1956. Also I thank historian

Donald C. Davidson for providing information about the Indianapolis 500 Mile Race. Errors are mine, not theirs. I thank Orion Crawford for remembering so much and for going after all those errant throws back then. I confess, they were uncatchable. I thank Grace Hine for every decent topic sentence I have ever written.

I thank researcher and author Gabriel Schechter of the National Baseball Hall of Fame for enormous help throughout this project, and Jeremy Jones of the Hall's staff for providing video footage of 1952 World Series games. Special thanks to Doak Ewing, founder and president of Rare Sportsfilms, Inc., for explaining the paucity of World Series game films from the early years.

Thanks to my friend and agent Philip Spitzer for realizing that this book was meant for George Gibson of Walker & Company, who has treated it so well. It is a joy to know and work with both of you.

I thank my parents for clear memories and loving support, and for managing to survive these events of fifty years ago and so much that came later. Thanks to my uncles Tom Brown and Lynwood Brown and my cousin Mike Johnson for sharing family stories with me. I appreciate Tim Hoose, the best of brothers, born just an inning too late to share this story with me. I thank Hannah Hoose for interrupting her studies to listen to chapter drafts over the phone, and Ruby Hoose for making the last few major-league and Sea Dogs baseball seasons so special for me. They are wonderful daughters. Sandi Ste. George shared the creation of this book with me more closely than anyone else, letting me read draft after draft to her, and offering the finest forms of encouragement. I hope she knows how much I appreciate her.

I thank Corrine Larsen for welcoming me to her home and for her kindness over the years. Finally and above all, I thank Don Larsen. Of course, like countless others, I thank him for the perfect game, which continues to amaze and inspire me. I thank him for his consistent generosity over the years, documented here. Above all, I thank him for throwing me a lifeline so long ago, even if he didn't fully realize he was doing so. To me, those gestures were the most important pitches of his career.